Less Is More

LESS IS MORE

A Practical Guide to
Maximizing the Space in Your Home

ELAINE LEWIS

Text with Judith Davidsen

VIKING
STUDIO
BOOKS

VIKING STUDIO BOOKS
Published by the Penguin Group
Penguin Books USA Inc., 375 Hudson Street,
New York, New York 10014, U.S.A.
Penguin Books Ltd, 27 Wrights Lane,
London W8 5TZ, England
Penguin Books Australia Ltd, Ringwood,
Victoria, Australia
Penguin Books Canada Ltd, 10 Alcorn Avenue,
Toronto, Ontario, Canada M4V 3B2
Penguin Books (N.Z.) Ltd, 182-190 Wairau Road,
Auckland 10, New Zealand

Penguin Books Ltd, Registered Offices:
Harmondsworth, Middlesex, England

First published in 1995 by Viking Penguin,
a division of Penguin Books USA Inc.

1 3 5 7 9 10 8 6 4 2

ISBN 0670-84239-7

The photographs on the following pages are copyright Derrick & Love and are used by permission: 15, 19-21, 26-34, 38, 40, 41, 51, 57, 58, 67, 98, 104, 105, 109, 110, 112-114, 116-118, 124, 125, 129, 132, 137, 139, 147, 149-152, 155, 157, 159, 162, 170, 172, 174, 180, 187, 189-191, 202, 203.

The photographs on the following pages are by Peter Paige Photography: 22, 25, 36, 45, 53, 55, 61, 62, 64, 69-71, 75, 89, 90, 93, 95, 96, 108, 122, 126, 128, 130, 131, 133-136, 142-144, 158, 160, 161, 168, 169, 171, 173, 175, 178-194.

The photographs on the following pages are copyright Elaine Lewis and are by Claudio A. Vasquez: 39, 43, 44, 46, 48, 49, 60, 63, 72, 78, 80, 81, 84, 86, 121, 127, 148, 153, 154, 176, 177, 184-186, 188, 192, 193, 195, 196, 198-201.

CIP data available

Printed in Singapore
Set in ITC Century and Bodoni
Designed by Kate Nichols

To my mother, Rose, and my father, Jack H. Kuperman.

Rose—we really did it!

Contents

Acknowledgments

I would like to thank Allen Gutwirth, who inspired me to write this book and then made sure I did, and Terrence Goldsack, whose creativity lives on even though he is gone.

The following people also helped make this book a reality: Judith Davidsen, High Voltage, Mel Berger, Barbara Williams, Dennis Sang, Jack Rosen, Nabeel Zahran, Maureen Fullam, Danny Cazzorla, Jeffrey Martin, and Shelley Ackerman.

Introduction

This book has been written primarily for all those people who feel they can't afford homes large enough to fit their needs or their decorating tastes. But even people who are lucky enough to have plenty of space can use this book to be sure they are making the most of what they have.

Over the past twenty or thirty years the price of housing has increased rapidly, yet all those extra dollars—which it now takes two incomes to supply—seem to buy us smaller and smaller spaces. Some of the more recent would-be luxury developments offer us interesting exteriors or marble bathrooms, but the bedrooms, for instance, are not much larger than those in old-fashioned public housing projects. In magazine after magazine we find house plans that eliminate both living room and family room and substitute a space called the great room that is the same size or even smaller than either room would have been ten years ago. Large structural columns break up the space in almost all the rooms in high-rise apartments. While older homes may be larger overall, they tend to be short on bathrooms; many are just large collections of small rooms.

In recent years, housing needs have changed even more profoundly, as more established households discovered they couldn't afford new homes or that the ones available were not much of an improvement, as the baby boom generation decided it was time for commitment, permanence, even babies of their own, and as people of all ages began establishing businesses in their homes. At the same time, increasingly stringent zoning and environmental legislation in some areas of the country have made many home renovation projects problematic. Today it seems everyone needs space that just doesn't exist.

As an interior designer and space planner, I have spent my entire career developing the skills that make it possible to create space out of almost nothing. Whether I design residences for Fortune 500 clients or for students in studios, my space-making techniques are identical. At the same time that I was creating luxury homes for people like John McEnroe, Eartha Kitt, the Rolling Stones, Tom Jones, and Sidney Poitier, I was also designing model homes and apartments to help developers attract buyers to increasingly smaller homes with smaller, and often oddly shaped, rooms. These models were incredibly successful in proving that any space—no matter how small or how strangely configured—has the potential to look bigger than it is and accommodate more furniture and storage than most people could imagine possible. The lessons those models taught the new buyers, and a lot more, are now contained between the covers of this book. The "Getting Started" section will teach you how to use easy professional planning techniques to organize your design ideas. Part One of the book will lead you on a room-by-room tour that describes space-enhancing design ideas for every room. Part Two is filled with instructions on how to use specific materials in specific locations to create the greatest amount of real and illusionary space. The Appendix deals with the design professionals, trades, fabricators, and vendors that you will encounter as you carry out your plans. The Resources section is a guide to the major manufacturers and retail sources in the interior design marketplace.

Throughout the book I stress that good taste has nothing to do with money and everything to do with making conscious and deliberate decisions about how you use the resources you have to create the home that fits your needs and gives you pleasure. My hope is that as you study the photographs you will begin to realize that creating the impressions you want at home depends on analysis and technique rather than on the ability to buy all the objects you see.

Remember that a well-planned home:

- Doesn't need a lot of costly objects—just the ones you love in a setting where you can enjoy them.
- Doesn't depend on small-scale furnishings—you can still have bold art, overstuffed chairs, and big four-poster beds.
- Doesn't depend on massive storage units—storage can be carved out of almost anything that can be measured in cubic inches.
- Doesn't depend on stark white walls—you can have moldings, wainscoting, dados, murals, and all the other period details that have become familiar through travel, museums, and even movies.
- Isn't limited to the actual space between your walls—color combinations, textures, and furniture placement can work together to create the illusion of space that isn't really there.
- Doesn't depend on expensive services by design professionals—this book will show you how to do it yourself. But even if you plan to go directly to a design professional, the book will help you know what to ask for.

Getting Started

Space planning calls for lots of list making. For the best results, get the entire household (along with any regular cleaning help) involved in the lists, especially the early ones outlining complaints and desires. Just make sure everyone understands these lists are meant to profile the household as it actually is, not what you—or magazines or developers—think it should be.

- Make a list of all the space problems you have in your home or a home you are considering moving to.
- Make a separate "wish list" covering everything you want, whether you have room for it or not. Washing machine? Four-poster bed? Twice as much storage as you have now? Big fat armchairs? Formal dining? Another bathroom? A grand piano? An exercise room? No matter how impossible it seems, write it all down.
- Go down the second list and check off all the wishes that you think you are going to have to sacrifice to space considerations, or visual considerations, or budget considerations, or considerations of practicality.
- If you haven't done so already, browse through this book, scanning the photo captions and the sidebars, all of which are full of ideas on how to avoid sacrificing what you want. Pay special attention to the pictures that don't particularly appeal to you—we live in a culture that tells us we can solve any problem by buying something, and the rooms that attract us seem filled with objects that tempt us to think that buying them will give us the same room, that tempt us to think we can quick-fix space problems by purchasing objects. It is much easier to learn space-planning techniques from rooms that don't distract us with objects; in the end it is those techniques that will let us make the most of the objects we love. (The more you study the pictures and their descriptions, the better you will become at figuring out how the rooms you see in other books, in magazines, and even in movies were created.)
- Then go back to your original lists and begin to notice how many of the sacrifices you thought you had to make turn out to be unnecessary, and how many of your desires you can fulfill after all.
- Finally, start planning, using the techniques listed below. As you plan, you will notice even more of your dreams can come true.
- Set up a filing system—with inexpensive colored file folders if you like—for floor plans, paint chips, fabric and wallpaper swatches, clips from magazines, ideas for separate rooms, even ideas for separate parts of rooms (for example, storage ideas, entertainment center ideas, furniture measurements and templates), and lists of trades and professionals and their estimates. (You can staple closed the ends of files that hold small pieces of

paper.) A box eight or nine inches deep should be more than adequate to hold all the files you may need, along with this book, and is small enough to move around to wherever you feel most comfortable doing your planning on any given day.

- Make yourself clear. Whether you are talking to housemates, to sales people, to designers, or only to yourself, avoid stereotypical but ultimately confusing terms like *masculine*, *feminine*, *romantic*, *hi-tech*; for example, the word *romantic* may mean lace ruffles and candlelight to you, but your listener is thinking zebra-striped satin. *Luxury* may mean intricately carved wood to you, and broad expanses of solid undecorated surfaces to someone else. *Modern* may mean absolutely up-to-date to you, and mean a fifty-year-old style to someone else. This is a waste of time. Use the most specific words you know ("I want it to remind people of lace ruffles but I don't want to use lace ruffles"), even when trying to describe an intangible effect. Try to find two or three ways of saying the same thing so you can reinforce your meaning without repeating yourself. Draw little sketches to show what you mean. Use pictures clipped from magazines. Encourage your listeners to respond in order to find out if you are all talking about the same thing.
- Design a room for your own pleasure and comfort. Forget about the neighbors, forget about the fashions shown in magazines and coffee-table books, forget about the developer's ideas of the "typical" family.
- A final note: The home that will give you the greatest pleasure is not necessarily the one that makes you say "Wow!" every time you open the door. "Wow!" could in fact be a warning signal that the space looks too much like a stage set, that it will turn you into an audience and demand that you pay it the kind of attention that no one should give to inanimate objects. Even actors are not at home on sets—that's where they put on an act to earn a living. You deserve something better.

How Can Your Home Serve You?

To help create a household profile and a wish list, think about these questions:

- How often to do you entertain? How often would you like to entertain? Do you prefer buffets or sit-down dinners? Dance parties? Do you have frequent drop-in guests? Entertain for business or volunteer organizations? In other words, are you looking for seating space, table space, floor space, quiet space, or combinations of these?
- Does your household enjoy spending long stretches of time together, or does everyone actually prefer privacy? Are there some members of your household whose bedrooms almost need to double as mini-homes?
- How much room do you need for exercising and exercise equipment? Remember that the floor space needed for a good stretching session (long enough for your height plus a few inches, wide enough for your arm span) may be more than that needed for an exercise machine and may need to be located right up against a wall.
- How many cooks are there in the household? How tall are they? Are they right-handed or left-handed? Who does the most cooking? Are there helpers in the kitchen at the same time? Who cleans up? Do you like guests to keep you company in the kitchen or do you prefer to cook in solitude? Do you cook simple meals or complex ones with lots of pots, pans, bowls, strainers, tools, and machines all in use at the same time? Are you a sloppy cook or a neat cook? Do you use especially large tools like lobster pots or canning equipment? Do you find that you don't use some equipment because you can't reach it easily? Is the dining room inconvenient for meals on the run? Would you like to be able to do other things—like paying bills or writing letters—while soup is simmering on the stove? Do you need a shelf for your cookbooks?
- Exactly what do you need to store? Skis? Down comforters? Power tools? Old LPs? Large serving trays? Mementos? Full-length gowns? Many of the objects we own have unusual dimensions and can be stored in unlikely places. You can, for instance, store toys in a hassock or skis in the plinth under the kitchen counters. The important thing is easy access, for, as a major closet manufacturer once said, "If you can't get at it you won't use it, and if you don't use it you don't own it. You're just storing it."

- Do you buy supplies in bulk or only as needed? Toilet paper? Canned goods? Olive oil? Paper towels? Shampoo? Computer paper? Powders for diet preparations? Breakfast cereals? Detergents?
- How much equipment do you need to keep on hand for household repairs and touch-ups?
- Do you have frequent overnight visitors? How much privacy do they need?
- Do you want a home security system?
- Do you have art, antiques, heirlooms, or collectibles that you want to display?
- How many functions do you want a room to fulfill? Before trying to fit them all in, make sure they don't conflict; for instance, in one household it might be possible for opera listeners and poker players to use the same room at the same time, while another household might take each activity so seriously that totally separate rooms would be required.

Know Your Home I

Finding out how your home was built can introduce you to hidden clusters of space you hadn't imagined could be there. The original architectural drawings are an obvious source that may be available from the developer or the local government agency responsible for building permits; double-check to see if changes were made during construction. You might also ask the previous owners, neighbors who have done renovations, or even contractors who have done work on identical units. If you have an older home, a local historical society may have some information on record even if the structure is not a landmark. If all these sources fail, you can hire a contractor on an hourly basis to investigate your home.

Once you have gathered together as many plans, drawings, and records as you can, you will need to look more closely at some crucial structural details in your home that will affect your space planning.

- Structural columns run from floor to ceiling and often jut into the room in the most inconvenient places. Because they hold up the structure or contain plumbing or heating risers, you usually can't get rid of them, but this book contains many techniques to camouflage them.
- Find the beams in your ceiling. You probably can't remove them, but the spaces between them can become part of the room's volume or can be kept covered and used to hold recessed downlighting equipment. The size of the downlights you buy will depend on the depth available between the ceiling and the floor above.
- If your home has concrete construction, ceilings and floors will be solid; for downlights you will have to use ceiling-mounted track (which has the advantage of letting you move the fixtures around) or recess the fixtures in built-in soffits or a dropped ceiling made of gypsum wallboard—as little as six inches will do.
- Electrical wiring can be moved easily, but you will need a licensed electrician who will get the necessary permits and arrange for a government inspection of the completed work; apartment dwellers may need permission from landlords or boards of directors. Apartment dwellers should also try to find out whether their wiring rises vertically from apartment to apartment (moving it could require shutting off the neighbors' electricity) or enters the apartment through a separate junction box.
- Locate the risers that carry plumbing, wiring, intercom systems, and ventilation ducts. Any room that backs onto a plumbing riser can use the pipes; for instance, a wet bar can be installed in a living room, or a mini-kitchen can be installed in a family room. Extra toilets must be attached only to toilet waste lines. Before getting too committed to extra toilets, check your local building codes; some localities try to limit toilets in order to avoid overburdening the environment.
- Find out the depths of the risers and how much of the depth is free for use as part of a room. You may be able to learn these dimensions by removing a medicine cabinet or a baseboard. Ventilation ducts may use up the entire riser.

Know Your Home II

Once you have a grasp of the construction of your home, try to look at the problem rooms objectively and ask yourself the following questions. Remember that many features you may perceive as liabilities can be turned into assets.

- How many square feet are in the room? What is its shape? Does it feel too narrow? Too shallow? Too boxy? How high is the ceiling? Where are the windows and doors? Structural pillars? Fireplace? Electrical outlets? Plumbing? Does a traffic route to other parts of your home pass through the room?
- Does the room have any especially attractive features, like a great view or a fireplace? Is this feature located where it attracts attention as soon as you enter the room, or will you have to find ways to direct attention to it? Do you own anything that you would like to make a focal point?
- How much natural light does the room receive? Do the windows seem too small or poorly placed? Do the windows admit glare or make you feel exposed, even though the view makes the room look larger? Is the view negligible? Horrible?
- Can you knock down a wall or part of a wall? Is it feasible to move doors or add windows? (Don't waste too much time planning major alterations until you find out if there are local codes or regulations governing them, or landlord or homeowner-association permissions for you to get.)
- Are structural pillars located where you can hide them inside bookcases or wall units?
- Can you hang a table off a wall to turn a foyer, a niche, or the end of a hall into a dining area or home office?
- Do any doors open onto things you'd rather not see, such as the toilet or the room of a perpetually messy person?

Creating a Physical Plan

Floor plans are the maps that keep you from getting lost in all the details of designing space. As organized physical pictures, floor plans show you possibilities that you might not have thought of. Elevations, or drawings of walls, can show you how your ideas will work out vertically. Models take a little time to build but can be invaluable for the many people who have a hard time combining the horizontal and the vertical into a 3-D picture in their minds. Whether you need to stretch an entire house or just the corner of a room, the more detailed your planning, the easier the actual job will be and the more satisfying the results will be.

Measuring

The first rule in planning is measure, measure, measure. As noted earlier, the original plans may have changed during construction. Even if you use one of the reasonably priced computer-aided design (CAD) programs available to consumers, you still will have to supply it with accurate measurements.

For the most accurate measurements use a heavy-duty carpenter's tape measure. Accuracy is absolutely critical to avoid false assumptions and purchases that are too big for the space or don't take full advantage of it.

Measure and note width, length, height, depth—for instance, 36W, 72H, 24D. You might want to make a quick freehand drawing of the object you are measuring and label all the sides.

Keep a special file for measurements so that you don't have to keep remeasuring every time you think about your plans. Even if you don't use a CAD program, entering the measurements into your computer can help you keep them organized and secure—just don't throw away the paper you originally wrote the measurements on.

Floor Plans

To create a floor plan, you will need to convert your measurements to sizes that will let you draw accurately scaled wall lengths on a piece of paper. The most frequently used scale, because it is conveniently small but still easy to read, is $1/4$ inch equals one foot (which will permit an ordinary $8^1/2 \times 11$-inch sheet of paper to represent a 34×44-foot room). A cheap plastic scale ruler will do the conversions for you, so you can measure the drawing rather than measuring the room or its contents whenever you need quick information; the three-sided kind of ruler that looks like a foot-long, inch-wide pitched roof will give you measurements in six different scales, usually $1/16$, $1/8$, $1/4$, $1/2$, $3/16$, $3/32$, $3/4$, and one inch, each as a representation of one foot. (The furniture symbols in this section are drawn to $1/4$-inch scale; see those pages for directions on how to use a copy machine to scale them up or down to suit the scale of your floor plan. As long as you keep the originals intact, you can trim the copies to more resemble your real furniture. You may be able to buy furniture templates at $1/4$-inch scale, but these are not cheap.)

Other essential supplies include a frequently sharpened number 2 pencil and the only brand-name product you will find recommended in this book, a Staedtler Mars plastic eraser, which gives the quickest, cleanest erasures I know of.

Use the symbols on the following pages to indicate load-bearing walls, structural columns, plumbing connections, electrical outlets and switches, door swings, and radiators.

Once you have all the data accurately drawn to scale, make ten or twenty photocopies so that you can test, with pencil, eraser, and white-out, as many ideas as you want for furniture arrangement, wall removal, sight lines, flooring installations, traffic patterns, and the like. (This is the fun part and you may find you prefer it to reading or watching TV.) Using photocopies of the furniture symbols on the following pages, or any other templates you prefer, start moving objects around on the floor plan. Use masking tape or art tape (more expensive, but it comes in narrower widths) to hold furniture symbols in place; avoid cellophane tape, which is more likely to tear the paper when you try to move things.

Keep in mind the following standard dimensions (check the kitchen and bathroom chapters for other specifics on fixtures and equipment):

- All closets, even those with sliding doors and hence no door swing, need a space at least 30 inches deep in front of them so a person can stand back a bit to get a decent view of the contents. Closets should be at least 24 inches deep, allowing 12 inches on either side of the rod.
- The front of a dresser should be 30 inches away from other furniture to make room for people to stand in front of open drawers.
- Figure at least 30 inches for traffic routes that pass between pieces of furniture.

- There should be at least 36 inches of walking space between kitchen counters.
- The space between a sofa and a small coffee table should be 15 inches; a long coffee table will require 24 inches.
- The space between a dining table and a wall should be 36 inches to allow moving a chair in and out; if the space is also a traffic route, plan 42 inches to accommodate both seated and walking people. Each place setting requires 24 to 30 inches of width.
- Most interior doors are 30 inches wide, but many bathroom doors are only 24 inches wide. Doors to the outdoors or to public halls tend to be about 36 inches wide.

Elevations

An elevation is simply a scale drawing of a wall, with doors, windows, art, moldings, built-ins, and the like drawn in, and perhaps color and pattern added. For a completely accurate view of the wall as it might be seen from the center of the room or from a door, however, the elevation would need to be drawn in perspective; unless you already possess that skill, it might be easier to build a model.

Models

Building a model starts out boringly, with the transfer of scaled measurements to an inexpensive sheet of foam core (available at art supply stores) and then cutting the sheet into floors and walls. A mat knife is the easiest cutting tool to work with; look for one with retractable snap-off blades and *never* let yourself put it down without first retracting the blade. Use the scraps for building structural columns, closet doors, built-ins, and the like.

Since foam core is about $1/4$ inch thick, it would perfectly indicate a 3-inch-thick wall in a 1-inch scale model; in smaller models, use $1/16$-inch Bainbridge board (available at art supply stores) for interior partitions to avoid throwing your room scale off. As the walls begin to build up from the foam core floor, you will feel your excitement mounting—you have become a builder! Stick glue is the easiest way to join the pieces, but add a few straight pins or masking tape in case the glue dries out before you are finished using the model (pins with T-shaped tops are easier on the thumbs). Attach one wall of the model just with a hinge of masking tape, so that you can open it for an eye-level view, and hold it closed with a pin. Use masking tape hinges for doors. Use pins or masking tape to install built-ins and walls you are not quite sure you want to remove.

When you are finished with the model, hang on to the larger pieces of foam core to use as protective underlays when you have other cutting jobs; a piece as small as 12×24 inches also makes a neat little lap desk that will last several months.

Mind over Matter

Once you've learned all you possibly can about the physical properties of your home and the objects it contains, it's time to deal with what may be the most crucial aspect of stretching the rooms you live in—how to create the *illusion* of space.

Illusion is a matter of fooling the eye, an organ that has tremendous power over the mind. While your measurements and your sense of touch will tell you exactly where a wall is, if you cover it with a pale or cool color, your eye will perceive it as farther away and convince your mind that the room has grown larger. If you direct light to a specific spot on a wall, the color there will appear paler and seem to recede. If your wall treatment has a layered effect—a trellis-pattern wallpaper, for instance, or a spattered paint design—the wall will take on a feeling of depth that will also make it appear farther away. If you mirror the wall, your eye will convince your mind that the wall has disappeared, revealing another space of the same size behind it.

By the same token, the longer it takes the eye to journey through a space, the larger the space registers in the mind. If you can move your eye along a diagonal line—through a flooring pattern, for instance, or the placement of accent colors—your eye will ignore the length of the walls and register the distance of the diagonal. If you arrange details so that your eye sweeps completely around the perimeter of a room from one point of interest to another, it will send a signal of very long distances to your mind. If your walls and carpet are the same

color, your eye will read the two as one large surface.

You may have been taught that hot colors, dark colors, and bold patterns can appear to pull surfaces toward you, but that doesn't mean you have to suppress your yearning for walls of brilliant orange or rich dark green, or boldly patterned wallpaper. An accent in a paler tone can function like a star in the night sky, drawing such attention to itself that the surrounding space seems infinite. A series of lighter tones—pictures, sculpture, light fixtures, upholstery, window or door trim—arranged on or right in front of a bold or dark wall will lead your eye on a long journey from object to object, while it registers the wall as something quite rich and satisfying but very much in the background.

Conversely, if you hang a sumptuous chandelier from the middle of the ceiling, your eye may stop there, enthralled, and never register the space in the other half of the room. Obviously, if you stop to think about it, you *know* that the rest of the room is there, but if your eye is not interested in the rest of the room, your mind is just not going to pay any attention to it. If, however, you put the chandelier in a corner, the gaze will immediately move along the diagonal in order to enjoy it. Operating on the same principle, you can use big, soft upholstered furniture and oversize decorative objects as long as you keep them from drawing attention to the middle of a room.

Keeping large objects off to the side may not always work, however. Huge armoires and custom wall units, for instance, seem to give us storage space only by robbing us of floor space and even ceiling space, making a room feel that much smaller. Sacrificing a tiny bit of storage in order to lift the unit a few inches off the floor and end it a few inches below the ceiling can give enough of a hint of the wall behind the unit to restore the room to its original dimensions.

As you study the various ways the eye can be fooled, you may be tempted to think there is one technique that will solve all your problems, but it's very rare for one element to do the job on its own. Solutions work in combination—painting the walls white may do nothing for your room unless you also get that red area rug out of the center of the floor, train a light fixture to cast a glow on the ceiling, place some bold accents strategically around the edges of the room, and find the perfect spot for a large mirror. Even if you invest in the perfect built-in, you will still have to use lighting, flooring, texture, and color to keep it from taking over the room.

As you work with this book, don't expect all the illusionary techniques to come popping out of the pictures at you—immediately obvious technique is the design equivalent of a ventriloquist letting his lips move; if we can see the technique, we don't believe in the illusion.

Using this book may sound like a lot of work—and sometimes it will be—but the premise is very simple: first you carve out as much functional space as possible between your walls, and then you apply illusion to make the space look even bigger.

FURNITURE SYMBOLS

You can photocopy these drawings, cut out the pieces, shape them a bit to better resemble the shapes of your actual furniture, and move them around on a $1/4$-inch-scale floor plan to experiment with placement. If your floor plan is of a different scale, set the copier to the indicated percentages, bearing in mind that furniture templates smaller than $1/4$-inch scale can be hard to handle and easy to lose.

$1/16$-inch scale	= 25 percent
$3/32$-inch scale	= 37.5 percent
$1/8$-inch scale	= 50 percent
$3/16$-inch scale	= 75 percent
$1/4$-inch scale	= 100 percent (or one-to-one)
$1/2$-inch scale	= 200 percent
$3/4$-inch scale	= 300 percent
one-inch scale	= 400 percent

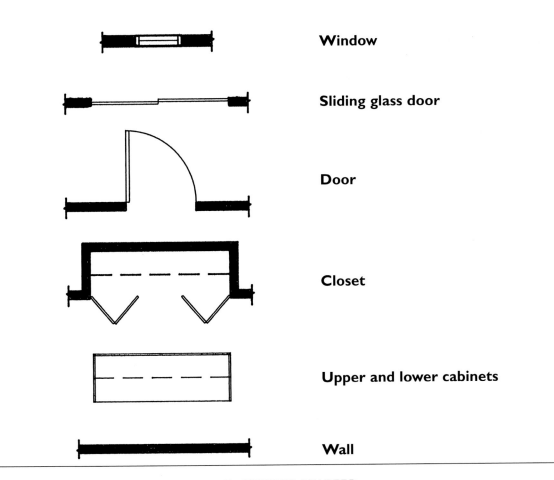

Window

Sliding glass door

Door

Closet

Upper and lower cabinets

Wall

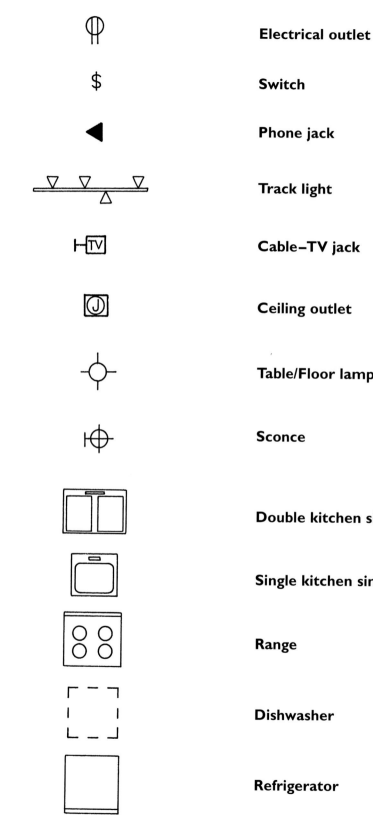

Electrical outlet

Switch

Phone jack

Track light

Cable–TV jack

Ceiling outlet

Table/Floor lamp

Sconce

Double kitchen sink

Single kitchen sink

Range

Dishwasher

Refrigerator

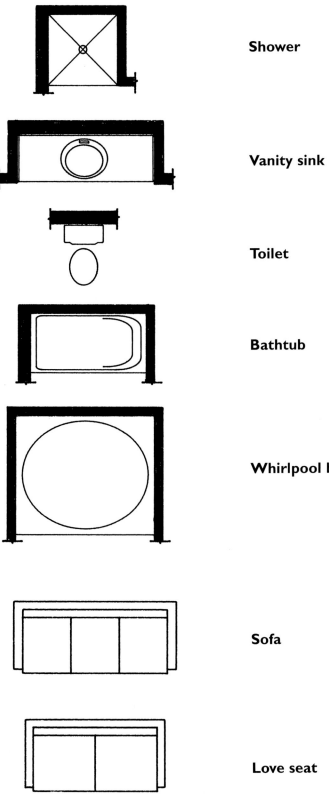

Shower

Vanity sink

Toilet

Bathtub

Whirlpool bath

Sofa

Love seat

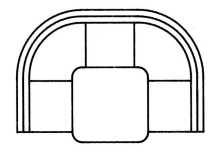

Banquette

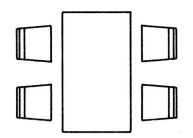

Chair and ottoman

Dining table and chairs

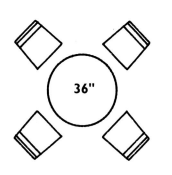

36"

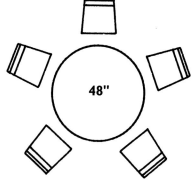

48"

**Circular dining tables
and chairs**

Potted plants

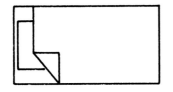

39" twin size bed

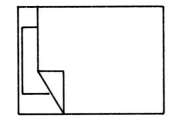

54" full size bed

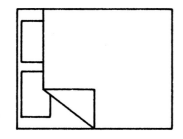

60" queen size bed

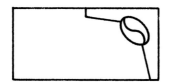

78" king size bed

Chaise longue

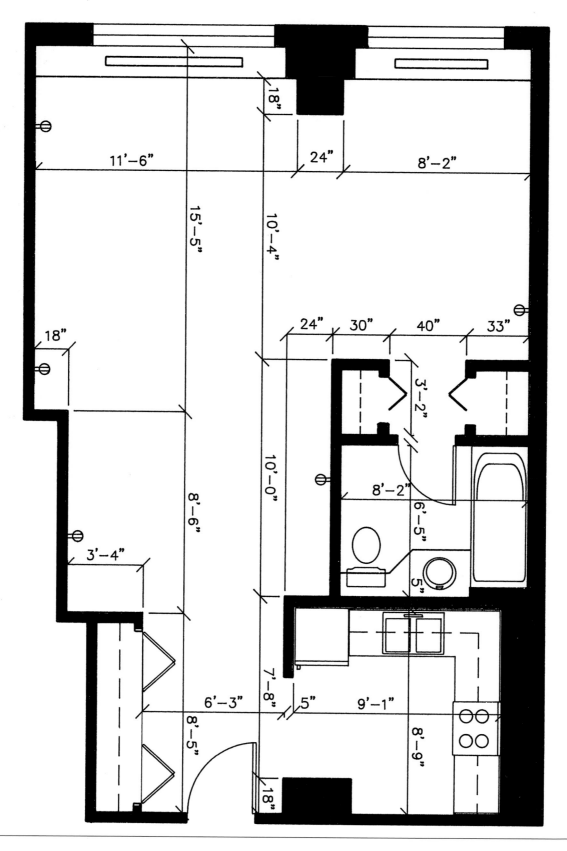

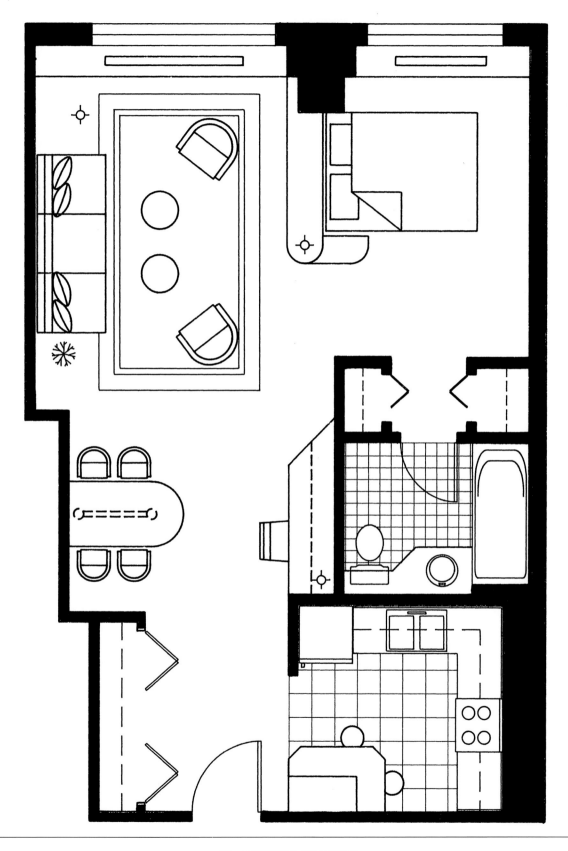

PART ONE

Living and Dining Rooms

Living rooms, dining rooms, and the modern open-plan living/dining rooms are the most public spaces in our homes. We can let ourselves go and relax completely in almost any other room, but in the living room and dining room we try to put on our best faces, not only to show respect for others but to demand it for ourselves. We will let most people this far—and no farther—into our homes and lives.

In homes without separate family rooms, the living/dining area can seem a bit schizophrenic. On the one hand we feel we have to impress people, even overwhelm them, yet these rooms are also at the center of our ordinary day-to-day lives. All the spare-time paraphernalia of the entire household tend to collect in the living/dining room. Private family activities seem to be at constant odds with public elegance and refinement.

Part of the problem arises from the origins of living and dining rooms. Centuries ago in Europe royalty and nobility had formal spaces—audience rooms, reception rooms, drawing rooms, salons, banqueting halls—where, we assume, they led festive lives in fancy surroundings. Ordinary people have been aspiring to this sumptuous lifestyle ever since.

But aristocratic personal spaces were really not all that functional or comfortable. If a duke and duchess, for instance, wanted a quiet night at home, their dinner had to be served to them on a trestle table at the foot of the bed. Because the table, chairs, food, and implements had to be brought in from other parts of the castle, the meal was cold long before it reached them. Chats with friends took place in what was a tiny combination dressing room/bathroom.

The one thing that we *can* learn from the nobility of old is the uses of formality, because, perhaps more than any other room, the living/dining room needs a design that suggests how it is to be used. Guests especially need visual instructions—through changes in color or lighting, for instance—on what to expect and how to behave, or they will feel uncomfortable. It may sound ridiculously petty, but simply knowing where the living room area ends and the dining area begins can go a long way toward putting guests at ease and letting them feel they belong; they need to automatically understand the space.

Clearly, a living/dining room that provides a welcoming space for visitors and protects them from a sense of free-floating chaos should work just as well for intimates who just want to eat pizza together in front of the television set.

A formal approach to living/dining room planning depends on finding ways to delineate where one activity area ends and another begins, without erecting walls or other barriers to spaciousness. Separating the dining area is especially important. A sit-down dinner is probably the most precisely ordered activity that can take place in a home. By comparison, even the most elegant living room activities are meant to be fluid and relaxed, a spirit that can be undermined if the dining mood seems to dominate the entire space.

It is also possible to announce the function of the furniture in a room, through subtle differences in color, texture, and size. A chair to be used mainly for reading or listening to music can be arranged with all the others, but might have a higher back or its own end table.

Desk areas within a living room also deserve some visual separation—a large lamp on the end of the desk might be enough to separate it from the group—unless the user doesn't mind being distracted or interrupted.

In many cases, a room will be divided naturally along an imaginary but powerful line between the entrance and an irresistible focal point like a fireplace or a spectacular outdoor view. The line between an entrance and an exit on an opposing wall is equally strong, if only because the eye recognizes it as a traffic route. Granted, these lines are imaginary, but they have great influence on how we perceive space. One way to separate dining and living room areas is to take advantage of these natural room divisions.

On the other hand, architects and developers often assign a certain spot for a dining area—they mark it as such on the sales plans and put an electrical outlet in the center of the ceiling—but the route to the kitchen may slice a corner off the living room, as seen in the diagram on page 23; people on either side of the line will feel far apart from one another. Take advantage of the division to install a desk or quiet conversation area in that corner, or get rid of the division by putting the dining area in the corner and letting the living room flow into the former designated dining space.

Other divisions may be more subtle. Even if the line from a door to a focal point creates an unusable demarcation line, a focal point is a powerful magnet for furniture groupings. For instance, a fireplace seems naturally to attract seating arrangements. The area outside the circle of furniture around the fireplace becomes the dining room; any space that falls outside the orbit of both areas can become a bar or service station, a mini-library or an indoor garden.

Even a room without obvious divisions often hints at possibilities. For instance, alcoves, corners, and the short legs of L-shaped rooms make natural dining areas, even when they seem too small. Pushing one of the narrow ends of a dining table flush to a wall can add

QUICK-CHANGE ARTISTRY FOR TELEVISION SETS

In most homes, the TV is the focal point of the living room, simply because common sense says to place it where the largest number of people can see it. Yet few of us consider a blank screen to be attractive or want to tempt guests to turn on sports events during formal gatherings.

A television set tucked into a wall unit is concealed or revealed simply by opening or closing a small door. To avoid having a blank door become the focal point, try hanging a lightweight piece of art on it, preferably something with a sense of perspective, or a layered pattern or raised design.

Television sets (and computer monitors) also can be permanently installed on mechanical pop-up devices in end tables or other low forms of cabinetry.

A truly simple solution is to leave the television set in full view, but placed only 18 to 24 inches above the floor. Then the TV is easy to ignore for people who are conversing standing, but at an ergonomically correct height for those who are actually viewing. Experts tell us that a TV positioned *below* eye level puts the least strain on eye and neck muscles.

Just remember that the old trick of whisking the TV out of the room on a trolley doesn't work anymore, because too much of our other audio/video/cable equipment is now hooked up to the set.

two feet, the space normally needed to push a chair out and in, and can make the table a perfect visual and physical fit for the space (see page 23). Rounding the opposite end of the table and supporting it on a single column will let you seat two at that end, compensating for the one seat lost at the wall.

Wall-hugging built-in banquette seating along one of the wider sides of a dining table can save space by eliminating the two feet needed behind each chair; a bench may do as well. But don't count on being able to move the table to help people slide in and out, especially if the table has a heavy base or the floor is carpeted; have a professional cabinetmaker install a mechanism that lets the table top slide without disturbing the base—or the table setting.

Drama in a Small Space

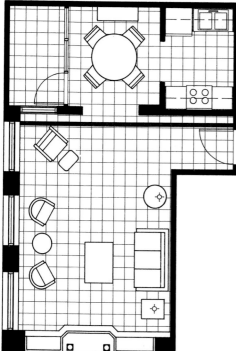

The owners of this home love large, dramatic decorating effects, but were stuck with a living room 12 feet wide and a dining area 9 by 10 feet. The spaciousness they were able to achieve is almost completely a matter of illusion.

BELOW: Silk-screened perspective scenes on the columns that frame the tiny dining area provide a great deal of visual stimulation without taking up any space at all and give the impression that the room boundaries could be miles away; a matte finish protects the scenes from smudges and wear. Cued to the sky in the landscapes, the pale blue painted walls and ceiling further blur boundaries inside the room. A simple pendant chandelier bounces light off the middle of the ceiling to reinforce the effect.

The focal point, at the far end of the shallow space, is a striking Arts and Crafts–style hutch, which seems to float against a wall of horizontal mirrors. This fool-the-eye technique works by riveting attention on a strong or bright object, thereby making the surrounding space seem endless. Open-work chair frames, a glass tabletop with a tree-form base that conveys a sense of bulk while maintaining an open form, and a mirror finish on the stone floor all contribute to the feeling of lightness and space. The mirrored radiator cover simply disappears.

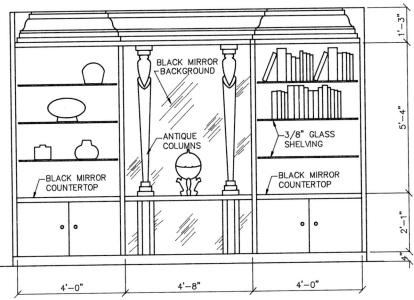

Living Room Wall Unit

Labels in the drawing:
BLACK MIRROR BACKGROUND
ANTIQUE COLUMNS
3/8" GLASS SHELVING
BLACK MIRROR COUNTERTOP
BLACK MIRROR COUNTERTOP

1'−3"
5'−4"
2'−1"
4"

4'−0"   4'−8"   4'−0"

FACING PAGE: A large custom wall unit immediately draws the eye to the far end of the living room. A black-mirrored central section lends a sense of perspective without actually reflecting the room; lower storage cabinets have been eliminated in the midsection in order to emphasize height and draw the eye to a substantial crown molding. The clear-mirrored wall behind the large sofa gives the narrow room a more square appearance and makes it seem as if the sofa is in an alcove.

In a traditional design scheme there would be an area rug to create interest and softness, but area rugs tend to make rooms look smaller. Here, the stone floor's pattern creates wall-to-wall interest, and the voluminous balloon shades provide softness while maintaining an airy quality. Open-frame furnishings and the way the one bulky piece echoes the tones of the floor let the space spread out as far as it can go.

RIGHT: When one moves from the blue-toned dining area to the creamy living room, there is the exhilarating feeling of rising from deep water into sunlight. The three-inch black stripe in the floor further delineates the rooms and also creates the impression that the tiny dining area extends out farther than it really does.

DELICATE FABRICS AND FINE FINISHES

If the living/dining room is used for public as well as private gatherings, delicate fabrics and very fine finishes may not make sense; household members may feel restrained in the only place they can relax together. Delicate fabrics should be reserved for small objects, like pillow covers, throws, and ottomans, which, should they show signs of wear, can be put aside until the time and budget are right for recovering, or for drapes, which are relatively safe from wear and tear. Very fine finishes should be positioned out of traffic paths and, ideally, out of the vicinity of food and drink. Many wooden antiques, however, have already survived more use than any of us are likely to give them in one lifetime.

The L-Shaped Room

Most people automatically assume that an L-shaped living/dining room is capable of accommodating nothing more than a living room within its long leg and a dining area within its short leg. However, shaking up that assumption—by moving functions around a bit—can provide a needed extra room: a den that can double as a guest room when necessary but still be available and inviting during parties.

ABOVE: A generous windowed space for a new den/guest room appeared when the dining room was moved out of its traditional ell and into an ample portion of the living room that traffic patterns had already made unusable for living room purposes. (A glance at the floor plan shows that in the original scheme, the dining ell had been located inconveniently far from the kitchen.) Lighter than a wall and transmitting far more light, a shoji screen sliding on a heavy-duty ceiling track was installed to provide privacy for the new space when it is used as a den or guest room; to open up the ell again, most of the screen can be slid behind the mirrored wall of the new dining area. Large contrasting floor tiles set the dining area off from the rest of the main space and give it a more formal character. A dropped soffit, containing recessed lighting, echoes the shape of the tiled floor to reinforce the official boundaries of the dining area. A second dropped soffit helps restore a sense of length to the living room end of the space. Applying mirrored panels to the long living room wall, the column outside the den/guest room, and the dining area wall creates an infinite series of reflected rooms to offset any sense of cramping in what is basically three rooms in one.

To avoid traffic jams throughout the space, the dining table has been placed flush with the wall; its curved outer end allows an extra chair or two to be positioned there at mealtimes. The see-through surface of the table keeps this corner light and airy. The living room furnishings are deliberately simple and low-backed to let the eye include some of the outdoors in its perception of the room size. The valance over the window conceals the shade mechanism and also fools the eye by suggesting that the window stretches all the way to the ceiling.

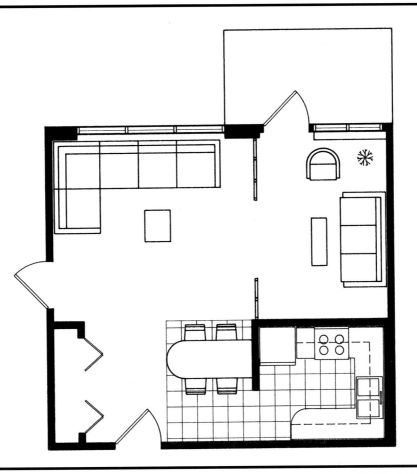

STORAGE—AND HIDING

In a home without a family room, it is especially important to create storage in the living/dining room for all the activities that will inevitably take place there. A built-in wall unit is an obvious choice for covering up the TV set on public occasions, as well as housing a small refrigerator, ice maker, and sink or bar, but there are other ideas you might want to consider; see "Built-ins" for suggestions on quickly hiding and retrieving such items as board and electronic games, books, personal computers, craft projects, mending, the main TV and stereo systems, and toys. Baskets and ottomans with hinged or removable lids are also helpful (some families keep outgrown toys in them for visiting children to use). Hints from "Family Rooms" also may be useful. Finally, for quick transitions from family-at-home to unexpected hosting, keep handy a large tray or small trolley for whisking away half-eaten snacks, used tissues, rumpled newspapers, shawls, odd shoes, and the like. The tray or trolley should complement the overall decor but not be crucial to it, since it probably will be out of sight for the duration of any surprise visit.

Inventing a Separate Dining Room

The challenge here was to create a place for formal sit-down dinners in a house lacking a separate dining room. The couple felt they could spare some space in the living room near the entrance, but they wanted to avoid a casual free flow of activities from one area to another; their decided preference was for formality. A wall could have given them two distinct rooms but would have destroyed the sense of spaciousness. The solution was to create a new floor level, one step up from the living room, which turned the "dining room" into a place unto itself.

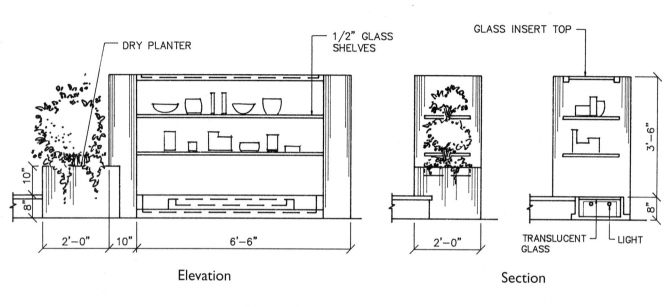

Elevation   Section

Living/Dining Room Step Unit

FACING PAGE: A custom-designed open unit, with glass shelves and a built-in planter, reinforces the division between dining area and living room without blocking visual flow; rounded corners ease the physical flow. The top of the unit can be used as a service station during meals, while the shelves below both store and display cherished serving pieces. A light fixture built into the base casts a glow upward through the shelves and top, adding a sense of airiness. Without this clear division, the Austrian shades and a brass-and-crystal chandelier would have seemed to be part of the somewhat more casually styled living room, and would have looked out of place.

The fireplace provides a focal point for the living room, and is surrounded by a warm peach-tinted mirrored wall that visually doubles the space and makes the large pieces of upholstered furniture, which were chosen for their well-padded comfort, seem perfectly proportionate. A large ottoman on casters provides extra seating, but can be rolled under the built-in console when not needed.

The hollow created by the coffee table relieves its bulk; the same principle of air and sight line flowing through an object applies to the sculpted ram next to the wing chair as well as to the open-shelf divider.

Putting Awkward Spaces to Good Use

The two windowed exposures that flood this living/dining room with natural light also created one of its drawbacks: limited wall space for storage or art. Another problem was that the opposite corner had been turned into wasted space by the traffic back and forth to the bedroom. Custom cabinetry fills the wasted corner with an entertainment center containing a television set that slides out and swivels to face either the living room or the dining area, and artful touches appear in unexpected places.

BELOW: Horizontal paneling covers the entertainment center and continues along the adjacent walls to unify, and at the same time to expand, the space.

Neon strip moldings in the tiny black-mirrored foyer and bedroom entry create a star-in-the-night-sky effect that, by drawing attention to brightness, gives the impression of unlimited surrounding spaces. The dining table is a work of art that doesn't need to take up limited wall space to be appreciated; it carries more than twenty coats of lacquer for durability.

ABOVE: The corner between the windows contains an awkward structural column now covered by three mirrored panels that capture extra light and unify the flow of windows. The neon construction, made from off-the-shelf tubes, creates a bright focal point in an otherwise neutral setting and seems to invite the occupant out to the terrace. The diagonal thrust of the column matches the diagonal shape of the entertainment center in the opposite corner.

On the principle that objects appear smaller the farther away they are, the flooring tiles start out large at the entry to the area and then, on the other side of the diagonal traffic-route border, switch to one fourth the size to make the living room area seem farther away than it is. The floor tiles also deliberately echo the diagonal shape of the corner structures. The spare lines of the metal-and-canvas side chairs cut down on visual as well as physical bulk, and allow the use of a large, well-padded sofa.

Selling Art from Home

This small living/dining room is not only a private home base but also a sales gallery for a fledgling dealer in Native American art and a space for entertaining clients. A number of techniques combine to permit one space to serve three purposes.

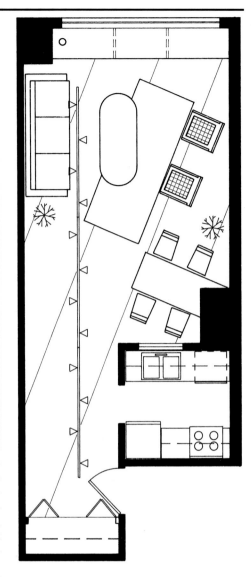

ABOVE: The tabletop, a piece of fossil-stone art supported by a single polished metal tube, cantilevers off the smoke-mirrored structural column on an angle to keep the dining area from crowding up against the kitchen wall. Both the kitchen pass-through and the cutout above it increase the sense of space but were also designed to comply with local building codes that prohibit windowless rooms. The bold custom clock turns the remaining horizontal strip of wall into a gallery space and prevents recognition of what it really is, the back of the kitchen cabinets.

The terrazzo floor, poured and polished on site, also follows a modest angle, which distracts from the enclosing parallel of the walls and directs the eye along the longest lines in the room, from one corner through the living room and dining area, past the kitchen to the mirrored bifold closet doors that give the impression that there is another large space just beyond.

FACING PAGE: A satin glaze over a spatter finish (see pages 140–162) gives a subtle sense of depth and continuity to walls, ceiling, and a custom radiator cover/bookcase in this room. Track lighting not only highlights art works on sale but also keeps surfaces uncluttered and available for changing displays (the small table lamp on the windowsill keeps the room from looking too obviously like a showroom). Open-frame rustic furniture lends texture to an otherwise very simple arrangement, and at the same time creates a sense of airiness by allowing the eye to travel under and through it. The same see-through principle makes the glass-top coffee table appear to take up far less space than it actually does. The long raw-silk hanging turns an otherwise intrusive structural column into a deliberate architectural element.

The Expanding Dining Area

This living/dining room came with all the hallmarks of graciousness—a bright curve of wraparound windows, an interior staircase leading to the bedroom floor, a double-height ceiling in one part of the room, with adjoining double-height patio windows—but it didn't have the kind of space the owners thought they needed for large-scale sit-down entertaining. Banquette seating turned a small dining area into a full dining room.

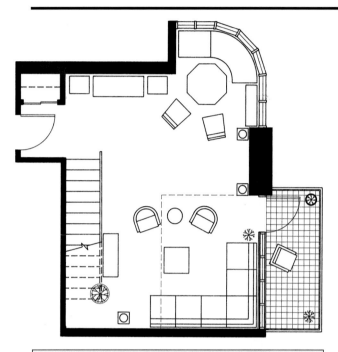

BELOW: The built-in banquette provides generous seating for three on one side of the octagonal table, while three individual chairs can be pulled up to the other side. With extension leaves, the table opens toward the living room area and can seat ten or twelve comfortably. Pale yellow upholstery, matching walls, center-column table base, and radiator cover (custom topped for use as a service station), along with open-frame pull-up chairs, help to maintain an airy solarium feeling. Since the center point of the dining area shifts as the table extends or closes up, a single swiveling track-head lamp, installed on an existing chandelier connection, can redirect the artificial light where needed.

The Corinthian columns visually mark off the dining area from the living room, while the mirrored wall behind them creates the illusion of additional windows.

STYLE VERSUS COMFORT

Don't let yourself get bogged down in the tug-of-war between comfort and style; you can have them both. For instance, a sofa, which we expect to be larger and bulkier than the other living room pieces, can provide well-padded comfort, while individual chairs can supply the drama and style. A chaise longue is just as comfortable as another form of recliner, but far more elegant and—more important—capable of being rendered in a wide variety of styles, ranging from boudoir-pretty to rustic and tweedy. If you tend to eat your dinner in front of the television set, a stylish coffee table, custom built two inches higher than usual, will make your meals far more comfortable but still be able to masquerade as nothing more than a coffee table.

ABOVE: To maximize the double height of the living room section, mirrors cover the horizontal beam that separates the lower and upper windows, making them appear to be one tall expanse of glass. The tree was chosen for its height and shape—it doesn't interfere with the view at eye level, while the delicate foliage, reflected in the mirror, appears to double in volume. The greenery actually takes up roughly one square foot of floor space. The centrally located tabletop crystal candelabrum does more than sparkle: light and airy, it continues the line of the tops of the armchairs to further delineate the living room area.

BELOW: The living room wall demonstrates the theory that there's no point in paying for double height if you are not going to flaunt it. The large abstract art form embraces the first- and second-floor sections of the wall in a position where framed art, no matter how large, might look simply adrift. (Framed art, on the other hand, seems to demand a closer connection to neighboring furniture, which normally means an eye-level placement that can begin to draw the walls forward.) The double rows of alabaster sconces draw the eye even farther upward, to highlight the impressive height of the ceiling; they also mimic, in material and thrust, the single marble column tucked under the balcony. This column visually extends the living room under the balcony and provides a formal ending to the long armless wraparound sofa that seats six in very generous comfort.

FOOL-THE-EYE TIPS

Color, texture, lighting, and changes in floor level can delineate different activities that take place within the same room, so that the needs of everyone—household members and guests alike—can be accommodated. For instance:

- Different flooring materials, in the same or contrasting shades, can create a formal dining area within a living room without the use of heavy enclosures.
- A collection of precious objects can serve as a focal point in even the most active room as long as special lighting effects (see pages 101–118) not only draw attention to the collection but also signal that the immediate vicinity—but only the immediate vicinity—requires somewhat more disciplined behavior.
- Raised floors and dropped soffits define separate activity areas without intruding on the fluidity of the space. Changes in floor level should be clearly marked and well lit.
- Low open-shelf units can divide rooms physically and provide storage and display space for books or precious objects, yet still maintain a visual sense of continuity. An open-shelf unit can also be used as a dining-area boundary, which has the added benefit of enabling the host to serve most of a meal from its shelves without leaving the table. Make sure the shelves are heat resistant and easy to wipe off, and consider installing roll-top doors to conceal the messy aftermath of a meal.
- A single piece of framed art hung at eye level can make a room look smaller by seeming to pull in the wall. A grouping of several smaller pieces, on the other hand, can make a room look bigger; the art will appear to float freely on a slightly recessed background.
- Furniture that reaches all the way to the floor cuts off visual flow; open frames and slender legs let sight lines pass through them. Furnishings raised only an inch or two off the floor can enlarge the sense of space in the room.
- Psychologically enlarge a room by erasing barriers between indoors and outdoors, not only by focusing on windows but also by using stone and brick wall treatments—faux or real— that hint at the outside of homes and make a room feel at least partially an extension of a larger world.
- Greenery arranged under windows helps to draw outdoor space inside. Within a room, large-leafed plants should be kept low to prevent their interfering with sight lines. Plants are useful for drawing the eye to—and blurring the transition from one wall to the other at—corners, for marking divisions between activity areas, for drawing out the length of a sofa, for softening the ending of a cabinet or sideboard. Ideally, tall plants should have thin trunks at eye level and light, delicate foliage above. In some cases, plants can function as architectural detail: bamboo, for instance, or the columnar forms of cactus and palm trees.
- Choose window coverings that allow a room to "breathe" and don't block views even as they establish privacy and protect from glare: mini- and micro-blinds, standard venetians, and shutters tilted partially down at the outside edge, simple sheer curtains, bamboo and split bamboo roll-ups, woven pleated shades, and pinhole solar shades. These treatments can be retracted quickly to expose a great landscape or skyline, or left in place permanently to conceal an undesirable one, while still suggesting there is something more out there (see pages 163–181).
- Those ugly structural columns that eat up space can be used to anchor design elements—bookcases, entertainment units, even dining tables. When put to work this way, they appear to be part of the flow of space instead of intrusions. Mirrored, they seem to decrease in bulk while making the surrounding space appear larger.
- Kitchen pass-throughs should be 36 or 42 inches above floor level to avoid exposing kitchen clutter and mess. If the pass-through is also a dining counter, use a 24-inch stool for a 36-inch-high surface, or a 30-inch stool for a 42-inch-high surface. Opening up space between upper cabinets and the ceiling increases the sense of airiness (and may be enough to satisfy local building-code requirements for ventilation in windowless kitchens).

Lighting a Cave

An entire wall of two-story-high windows bathes the living room end of this townhouse duplex in horizon-expanding light and views, making the dining room end, tucked under the bedroom balcony along with the kitchen, staircase, and entry, appear dark and cramped by comparison. A small textured wire-glass partition was installed to subtly separate the dining room from the more densely packed rear of the home and to connect it firmly with the airy living room. Light bouncing off the partition suggests at least subliminally that both ends of the space are windowed and have access to a wider world.

BELOW: To ensure that the wire-glass partition did not make the kitchen and entry feel even smaller than before, a pattern that echoes the living room upholstery was used on one of the entry walls to suggest that the larger, more airy space extends back toward the front door.

Open-back antique chairs occupy the room side of the table, while a banquette hugs the wall on the other, trimming the width of the dining area so well that it became possible to install an open-frame desk—which doubles as a sideboard—and chair against the opposite wall. The use of a bulky dining table is possible because its inverted pyramid base gives it a floating feeling and no corner obstructions if another diner wants to squeeze in.

LEFT: A large carpet from central Asia defines the living room—without the use of physical barriers—and visually connects the main conversational grouping to a second seating area, foreground, which is cut off physically by a traffic route to the dining room and kitchen; a smaller carpet might appear to take up less space, but it would attract attention to its size and pull the walls toward it.

The overstuffed sofa also lends a commanding presence to the living room, but its placement against a side wall prevents it from blocking the field of vision. The side chairs are dramatic enough to form a focal point, but their open framework permits sight lines to move through and around them to the terrace and the city beyond. Toward the entry end of the room the pieces are kept small and low to permit the eye to sail right over them. The mirrored column suggests that the room is roughly two windows wider than it actually is.

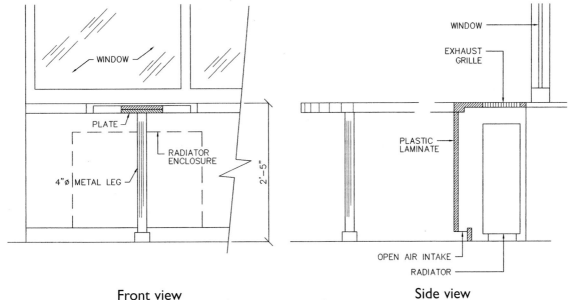

Front view

Side view

**Radiator Enclosure and
Dining Table Unit**

Cozy Corner

The owners of this small home wanted to use the open living/dining room area strictly for living room purposes, but the only place left for eating was a tiny corner off the hall. Only seven feet wide, the corner seemed barely big enough for a bistro table, let alone a formal set of table and chairs for comfortable sit-down entertaining. A large structural column created even more space problems. But what had turned the corner into a virtual cave became a major element in enlarging the space.

RIGHT: The structural column became incorporated into the design in order to anchor one end of a comfortably upholstered banquette. Open-back chairs in a light wood finish fill in the other side of the table, where there is room to move in and out. Because the structural column is now part of the seating arrangement, an end chair can extend along one side of it and slightly into the hallway.

A faux stone wall treatment gives the dining nook the feeling of an outdoor courtyard. The mirrored shelf displaying domestic objects provides an intimate counterpoint and echoes the horizontal thrust of the banquette upholstery below to make the area appear wider. Open-frame chairs and a glass-top table let the gaze travel as far as possible, while the pale color scheme makes the space appear larger.

Doubling the Drama

There was only one space available in this home for sit-down dining, but with its lack of serving space and its blank rear wall abruptly cutting short spectacular views, it conveyed a decidedly cramped impression. Mirroring the entire back wall and corner structural column not only doubled the appearance of the space but also permitted a gentle shift from outside drama to inside drama.

ABOVE: A pass-through punched into the kitchen wall provides a service counter and an extended view while concealing the messier kitchen operations from seated diners. On the opposite side of the dining area, more serving space is available on the top of a bookcase, whose surface is an extension of the windowsill. The same carpeting in the living room and dining area creates a sense of flow.

The custom-built bookcase slants back as it approaches the living room in order to create a more gracious transition to the dining area and ends in an abbreviated classical column that formally announces the shift from one room to the other. Sleek open-frame chairs keep the view uncluttered. The black metal framing on the mirrors echoes the window frames.

Family Rooms

Family rooms came into fashion after World War II, at a time when parents were encouraged to spend as much time as possible with their children. It was no longer enough to protect and discipline children—it now became important to play with them, work with them, and generally to enter into the world of childhood. The grown-up realm of the living room didn't seem quite the right place for this new family function, but neither did the small-scale domain of the nursery. Thus the family room was born, with its adult-size furnishings and childproofed finishes.

Today, family rooms are used for many different purposes. As a place for children (household members or visitors) to entertain themselves while the adults relax together in the living room, family rooms are ideal. But even in households without children, extensive entertaining for business, social, or political reasons may mean that relaxation and intimacy are possible only in a family room. A family room also becomes a necessity for people who set up home offices in the more impressive living room.

Unfortunately, some people think that a family room, in order to withstand constant use, has to be dark or drearily neutral. Worse, some think nothing of quality can survive in a family room, and haphazardly furnish it in worn-out castoffs from other rooms. Finally, some seem to think that because a family room has to serve so many different household members' needs, it must be large. None of this is true. A well-designed family room can be small and very attractive, and still accommodate a wide variety of activities.

Some developers have combined the living room and family room into something called a "great room," leaving some new households feeling that a special place is missing from their lives. Many turn the space into a family room and forget altogether about having a living room.

GLASS-TOP TABLES IN A FAMILY ROOM?

Glass tops create the illusion of more space by making tables disappear into their surroundings. If specified correctly, they can be as sturdy as any other solid surfaces. Use $1/2$- or $3/4$-inch glass supported around the edges with a wood or metal frame, or, if frameless, supported underneath with a pedestal design. Beveled edges and rounded corners prevent bruises and cuts. However, if you feel anxious about using glass tables around children, don't do it.

Safety glass may sound safe, but it tends to be thin and very expensive, and is designed for vertical uses like windows. Clear acrylic is very strong, but heavy use leads to scratching and cloudiness.

The Garage as Family Room

The young owners of this home originally wanted a family room with lots of flexible seating, along with full kitchen and eating facilities—a separate home within the home—but their house did not have enough room and local laws did not permit the extra plumbing needed for a second kitchen. The solution was to remove the wall between their existing kitchen and a small attached garage (because they live in a mild climate a carport was adequate housing for their vehicles).

ABOVE: The garage door was replaced by floor-to-ceiling windows that spill enough daylight toward the kitchen to remove the shadows that had plagued it for years. The far end of the kitchen continues to open directly into the more elegant living/dining room.

The new island contains the sink (a stove top in this position would be too dangerous) and is wide enough to do double duty as a snack bar; the stools are backless to avoid a cluttered look. The outer corners of the island are rounded to create the illusion of one long flowing line, and also to prevent injuries as children race around the island. The end closest to the breakfast nook can be used as a service station, as well as a work or dining surface. Where the counter joins the structural pillar, the counter was extended at an angle to create more work space. An upper cabinet, with doors accessible from both sides of the island, was attached to the pillar; it provides extra storage without blocking the view between kitchen and family room. *(continued)*

The bulkier installations—the pillar cabinet, the pantry with its louvered doors for air circulation, and the refrigerator—were clustered by the entry to keep the eating and working areas as continuously open as possible. To conserve work spaces, the combination microwave and stove vent is wall mounted over the traditional stove. Shallow cabinets for seldom-used equipment top both microwave and refrigerator. To keep the refrigerator from blocking views, it was moved from the sink side of the kitchen; its water supply for the ice and ice-water makers comes from the master bath on the other side of the wall.

ABOVE: Centrally placed in its own niche, the entertainment unit allows the TV to be viewed from the kitchen, breakfast nook, and family room, and was designed to accommodate a VCR, stereo rack, storage for video- and audiocassettes, a bottom drawer for video games, and a cubby hole for remotes and TV listings. Built-in seating hugs the wall and swings into an alcove created by the entertainment unit; mirrored, the alcove suggests additional space. Because it doesn't face the entertainment unit and is buffered by the unit's cabinetry and the wall of the niche, the alcove becomes the family room's quiet spot. A dropped soffit in the alcove houses downlights to keep the corner bright and airy and provide illumination for such activities as reading or mending without glare from the TV screen; a dimming system lets the lights be turned down for intimate conversation. White upholstery, the same color as the walls and floor, lets the seating bulk dissolve. The ottoman (on casters) helps to distinguish the eating area from the sitting area. Both sofa and ottoman cushions lift to reveal generous storage spaces for toys, sweaters and shawls, and mending. A tongue table pulled tight to the windows makes the dining area easier to get around and appear larger. The same vinyl tile was chosen for kitchen, breakfast nook, and seating area to enhance the sense of a continuous flow of space.

Grandparents Need Family Rooms Too

Over the years, the professional couple that owned this home had filled it with antiques and created an environment perfectly suited to their heavy schedule of business entertaining. But now they needed a special area where they could relax and entertain their most cherished visitors—their grandchildren, who live in the same neighborhood and drop by frequently. The style of the furnishings had to reflect the couple's taste for traditional free-standing pieces and their need for comfortable, well-cushioned seating. The new family room also had to fit into a small former bedroom.

ABOVE: The traditional armoire, which contains the TV and audio equipment, games, and an encyclopedia, has great mass, yet it manages to create two rooms out of one: on the near side, a chair protected from the sounds of the entertainment center provides a haven for reading and lap sitting, while the far side becomes a nook for snacks, homework, and board games; a small bookcase for storybooks nestles behind the table at the end of the long radiator cover.

The diagonal lines of the armoire's ends reduce its apparent mass without sacrificing very much storage space; hidden lighting fixtures let the shelves float. Using the space atop the armoire for large decorative objects draws the eye upward. At the window, the simple valance softens the stark modern-style wall/ceiling boundary and fools the eye into thinking that the glass extends all the way up. The diagonal rug pattern echoes the lines of the armoire and draws the eye to the farthest reach of the room, where the glow from an uplight floor lamp lends extra height to the ceiling. The light coffee table is easy to move when the sofa opens to accommodate the children when they stay overnight.

Multiple Activities in the Family Room

Built on a piece of sloping land, this house had a small segment of basement that was underground on one side but open to the outdoors on the other. The teens and young adults in this large family each wanted to claim the space for their own activities, and the politically active parents wanted a place where they could conduct meetings in casual surroundings. The existing structure of the basement suggested natural divisions into function areas.

ABOVE: Boldly painted structural and false beams and columns create the sense of many rooms in one, all with access to the daylight from the patio door: a bar/kitchen with a small sink, a microwave, and an ice-making refrigerator; a table area that can be cleared quickly for dancing; a quiet seating nook next to the kitchen; and another seating section (see drawing) in the more open area. The raised floor reinforces the sectioning as it also accommodates the kitchen plumbing; the gap between it and the main floor suggests additional space by letting the area float.

The pendant lamp lights the table for meals, buffet service, neighborhood meetings, and occasional paperwork, but can be looped out of the way on a hook for dancing parties; the table can be dismantled and temporarily stored when maximum floor room is needed. Since the table is close to the wall and not in a direct line with the patio doors, the pendant does not foreshorten any important sightlines. The picture on the wall lends a sense of perspective to the area; the storage chest underneath contains files, a calculator, a laptop computer, a portable printer, and a small fax machine.

Wall-mounted fixtures in the seating area provide good light for reading and studying without taking up surface space; they can be dimmed to conversation or party levels. A mirrored wall brings light and color into the hall leading to the rest of the house.

PHYSICAL PLANNING

- Traditionally, family rooms have been placed near the kitchen to make it easy to get snacks and drinks, and to let parents exercise some supervision while they are cooking. A better idea is a pass-through between kitchen and family room so that views continue into the second room and the adults become more available to the children.

  Warning: Never install a cooktop in the pass-through between kitchen and family room; it is too tempting for someone to reach over it and risk getting burned. A sink is ideal, since it can be used safely from either side of the counter.

- If you have to go into the basement to create a family room, plan your kitchen facilities around the water and waste lines from a bath or kitchen above. If that's not possible, consider installing an old-fashioned dumb-waiter device to carry water between floors for ice and cleaning, and stock plenty of bottled water in the refrigerator. At a minimum, a family room kitchen should have a small refrigerator with a freezer compartment for ice cubes and snacks, a small microwave, and a two-foot-square surface for cutting and assembling snacks.

- To provide a round-the-clock welcome for every member of the household, the family room should be—or at least appear to be—as uncluttered as possible. Storage options include wall units with a variety of shelves, drawers, and doors; seating units, including ottomans, with storage bins under the cushions; chests or boxes as coffee and side tables, with casters for easy moving. Use locks on cabinetry that stores activities you want to keep regulated—TV, video games, an expensive chess set, inherited dolls; it's easier than saying no every five minutes.

- For a family room entered directly from the outside, create a small tile-floored area near the door, with pegs for outerwear and shelves for muddy boots, dry slippers, and some shawls or afghans.

- Because the family room gets such heavy use and contains the property of so many household members, it is not an ideal spot for adult sleep-overs.

- To keep surfaces clear for activity, use downlight, pendant, or wall fixtures for lighting; wall-hugging shelves for display; attractive baskets and boxes for activities that involve a large number of pieces of equipment; pop-up or pull-out devices for TVs and computer equipment. In a pinch, a TV can be hung on a wall; a globe can hung from the ceiling.

- Adjustable spotlights, rather than pendants, are a good choice over a table; for dancing or other activities the table can be moved without worrying that people will bang their heads into a light fixture.

- Choose lightweight furniture or furniture equipped with casters for the family room. This will enable you to clear the floor quickly for lounging, games, and parties. Look for a table with a removable top and a pedestal or collapsible base or have one made.

- Resist the temptation to keep all the seating together in the family room. Instead, scatter activity areas so that small groupings can occur naturally. Keep at least one chair out of line with the TV.

- If there is absolutely no way to carve a separate family room out of your existing home, try creating family room niches throughout the house: an adult-size easy chair or love seat in a child's room; a surface—out of the line of the TV—that can be easily cleared for homework or board games in the living room; a bookcase and a couple of easy chairs at the end of a dining room or eat-in kitchen.

Breaking Down Barriers

When the owners of this home were growing up, family rooms were almost always separated by a wall from the kitchen; adults were on one side, children on the other. So they had some difficulty at first understanding how much more functional, comfortable, and attractive an open-plan kitchen/family room could be. Removing the walls that separated the kitchen from the family room enabled these parents to attend to kitchen chores while being fully available to their children.

ABOVE: Sliding doors provide a clear, unobstructed view to the outside, facilitating parental supervision of the yard. Inside, they can even watch the TV, which swivels out from the storage unit on the right—although these parents are very careful to always stay outside when the children are in the pool. The countertop in the kitchen is wide enough to function as a snack bar as well as food preparation area.

Surfaces less prone to wear—cabinetry, walls, window treatment, and floor—are white, which makes them seem to recede and expand the space. The more easily damaged seating pieces are in dark, vibrant tones, accented with white pillows that have washable covers. To withstand the constant traffic of wet feet, the floor is vinyl tile. A commercial-grade, low-loop carpet with a painted pattern adds a residential look; positioned on the diagonal, it leads the eye along the longest line in the room.

The patio door was reversed in order to locate the sliding panel on the same side as the traffic path through the room to the kitchen and the rest of the house. Hugging the wall and the stationary panel (but not blocking views) is a low-slung sectional sofa. A large unframed mirror over the sofa makes the wall seem less of a boundary. The mass of the entertainment center is located on a wall that does not immediately attract the attention of anyone entering the room. The low, dark easy chair swivels so that anyone sitting there can watch TV, talk to the cook, or join the main seated group without moving any furniture. The collection of small coffee tables moves quite easily so that the sofa can open for sleep-overs.

A small section at the end of the adjoining bedroom closet was equipped with a ventilated louvered door to hold towels and pool maintenance equipment.

Kitchen-in-a-Closet

This family wanted a quiet gathering place away from both the formality of their living/dining room and the hurly-burly of their children's activities. They also wanted to be able to serve up snacks and quick meals—burgers, eggs, pizza, and sandwiches—to family and friends without giving up the space required for a full kitchen. A Pullman kitchen was installed on the other side of the wall from the existing full-scale kitchen and shares plumbing and electrical lines with it.

BELOW: The Pullman arrangement is a single 24-inch-deep row containing a two-burner stove top, a small sink, and a refrigerator/ice maker, with some counter space below and a row of cabinets and a wall-mounted microwave above. The appliances and cabinetry are directly behind the ventilated louvered doors; the cook actually stands in the family room while using them.

The wall unit contains a TV, a dry bar, display space above, storage below, and recessed downlights to balance the light from the window and let the entire wall appear to move outward. To connect the cabinetry at the far end of the room, the wall unit extends under the window as a radiator cover/extra seating, and partway up the other side of the wall as closed storage. A large-scale graphic rug was chosen to deemphasize the mass of the coffee table. The white sofa on one side and patterned armchairs on the

other draw attention away from the center of the room and help to push the walls outward; the legginess of the chairs also helps to open up the most tightly packed part of the room.

The dining chairs are small in scale, but upholstered to appear substantial and lend a hint of formality. Since the eating area is lit by an adjustable ceiling spot rather than by a stationary pendant, the table can be moved around at will, or dismantled and stored when large expanses of floor space are needed for parties.

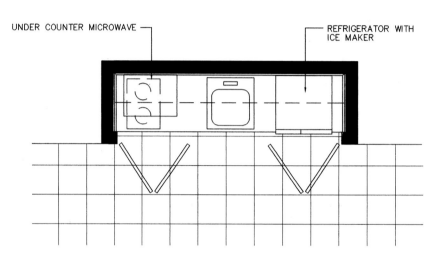

UNDER COUNTER MICROWAVE

REFRIGERATOR WITH ICE MAKER

Pullman Kitchen

DURABLE DOES NOT MEAN DULL

- Laminates come in every conceivable color, texture, and pattern. Nowadays, even the palest are resistant to staining; not even grape juice or tomato sauce leaves a mark. Laminates with fine pebbly finishes tend to hide scratches and fingerprints best. If you worry that laminates look like phony wood or stone, remember that most of them consist of color and abstract pattern and aren't designed to resemble any particular material.
- Sturdy upholsteries, such as tapestries and canvases, are available in a wide variety of patterns and colors, and are very well suited to heavy use in a family room. Patio fabrics in vibrant colors are also ideal for brightening up family rooms. The commer-

cial upholstery fabric used for office furniture is extremely durable and becoming more and more residential in appearance. Called "contract fabric," it is available through professional upholsterers.
- Accent pillows and floor pillows can be covered with washable fabrics and zippered. Since they are easy and cheap to replace, pillows may not have to be as sturdy as upholstered pieces.
- Commercial carpeting is just about as sturdy as industrial-grade, but comes in a wide variety of colors, textures, and subtle patterns for use in upscale executive offices. Most carpet outlets sell both commercial and residential products.

From Junk Room to Family Room

This family had reached a point where the adults and teens were getting on one another's nerves, but no one liked the idea of using bedrooms as escape hatches—that would have made the bedrooms feel like exile. However, behind the under-house garage was a small enclosed space cut into a slope and fea- turing a strip of horizontal windows placed high in the back wall. At first glance, the room, filled with trunks and garden equipment, seemed too small for anything but storage, but a second look revealed that it could be turned into a cheerful, comfortable space for a variety of grown-up and teen activities.

ABOVE: Since the plumbing for the existing kitchen ex- tended downward next to the door to the basement room, a second kitchen was erected there, with a refrig- erator/ice maker and sink on the back wall and a cook- top under—and protected by—the pass-through. The pass-through and the open space above the top cabinets combine to keep the kitchen connected to the rest of the room, and also to satisfy local regulations that prohibit windowless walled-in rooms. On the other side of the entrance, a shelved walk-in closet stores the garden equipment and other paraphernalia that had formerly been strewn in one layer all over the basement room. Both kitchen and closet are clad in a cool color to help them recede; at the same time, the color's intensity en- sures that the eye is drawn as far as possible from the center of the room. Similarly, the bright throw pillows on the love seats keep the eye moving around the dis- tant edges of the room.

The table is a tongue shape pulled flush to the wall so that four can sit there, with two more at the rounded end; a freestanding table, requiring chair space on all sides, would not have fit here. The uplight floor lamp gives a lift to the ceiling and bounces illumination back down to both the table and the sofa. The two frameless round mirrors (see reflections) are so large that they seem to be wall openings giving on to more and more space beyond; through their sheer size, they also balance the kitchen mass without taking up any physical space of their own.

Peace and Quiet

As the children in this family entered the loud and boisterous stage, the parents realized that what was needed was a place for quiet—a place where both generations could watch TV programs or talk over problems or tackle homework together; where anyone coming home extra late from work or school could have a full hot meal within the family group instead of being isolated in the kitchen or dining room; a place where the parents could lounge or catch up on paperwork on the weekend while still keeping an eye on the comings and goings of their children, who had developed the habit of entering the house through the garage. The problem was that the house, small and built around 1950, wasn't built with a family room, and the household couldn't sacrifice any other room to create one. The solution was to convert the original garage into a family room, and build a new, larger garage next to it.

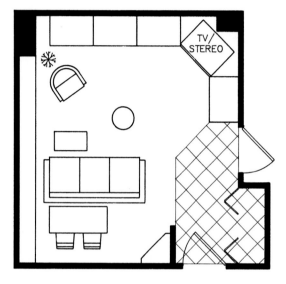

FACING PAGE: In the old garage, a new ceiling was laid on the overhead beams to create a storage space under the pitched roof; the beams were left exposed and painted the same color as the ceiling to create a layered sense of distance. Around the edges, dropped soffits contain recessed downlights.

The back wall is almost filled with custom cabinetry that holds a TV and stereo equipment, a VCR, tapes, puzzles and other quiet games, and mending, and, on the open shelves, books and display items. The visible wall surrounding the unit is mirrored to keep the front of the unit from appearing to be the end of the room. Under the windows, the radiator/air-conditioner cover extends across the wall to create a longer line for the eye to travel over and to incorporate more bookshelves; the brass lamps on the top shelf can be adjusted to tasks or, as seen here, to augment the downlights in pushing the walls outward. On the wall between the windows, an outdoor scene in recessive colors reinforces the outward push of the walls.

Aside from these built-ins, the rest of the furnishings are freestanding to make it easy to clear the floor for parties. Most of the time, however, the sofa, which faces the TV, divides the room. Generally, a bright bulky object centrally placed would pull the walls inward, but in this case the sofa is not a focal point and in fact faces away from the center toward the TV, helping to direct attention to the outer edges of the room, making it seem larger. Two people can eat full meals on the sofa table behind while also watching TV or participating in conversations. The corner wing chair is part of the conversational group, but is placed out of the direct line of the TV in case the occupant wants to read. Since the original garage opened into the kitchen, food and drink are always only a step away.

Since the family room retains the old garage side door to the outside, the children are now more likely to be greeted by family as they enter the house. A small mud area (see drawing) uses vinyl tile that matches the rug to connect the outside entrance to the kitchen door. A shallow closet between the two doors contains pegs for outerwear and shelves for muddy shoes and warm slippers.

FOOL-THE-EYE TIPS

- When a kitchen visible from a family room is not in use, keeping a light on above the sink helps to make the two areas appear to be one large space.
- A seating arrangement in either more vivid or more subdued tones than the rest of the family room can reinforce it as an area for special activities—for example, reserved for reading or quiet conversation.
- Exposed ceiling beams can be incorporated into a design in these ways: painted a bright contrasting color, they can appear to form a separate open-frame structure behind which the real ceiling seems to recede; painted the same color, they can make the ceiling float at an indeterminate height; either way, they can help delineate different activity areas.
- To establish a sense of flow throughout the more public rooms in the house, carry some design details from the living room and/or dining room into the family room. For instance, use the same color upholstery, but switch from silk in the living room to canvas in the family room. Switch from a plush carpet in the living room to the same color tile or commercial-grade carpet in the family room. Use similar window-treatment styles and colors, but in more casual materials, and the same furniture and cabinetry tones, but in laminate instead of wood.
- To give a lift to the ceiling, install fluorescents in a cove a few inches below it.

Bedrooms

All too often, we waste our time and energy trying to adjust ourselves to a bedroom rather than concentrating on making the room adapt to us. After all, we say, it's a private space, the door is closed, nobody ever sees it but us. We'd like it to be nice, but somehow all our best efforts seem to go into creating a welcoming environment in the more public areas of the house, the places that outsiders see and by which we are judged. We think we can postpone welcoming ourselves until some indefinite time in the future.

From the space-planning perspective, the bedroom has two main functions—it has to provide easy-to-reach storage for your clothes and, believe it or not, it has to make you really happy to be there.

It can, if you want, also perform as an office, or a reading room, or a sewing room, or an exercise room, or a homework room for a child who shares a bedroom with a noisy sibling, or a quasi–family room where everyone nestles in to watch TV together or chat. But if the room doesn't feel comfortable and pleasing—if, for instance, you stub your toes and bruise your thighs every time you try to get to your clothes or to an outlet for the vacuum cleaner, or if you don't like the colors or textures or furnishings that you chose—then this is a space that will make you feel small and insignificant no matter how big it really is.

Conversely, a room that pleases your eye and smooths your way as you move within it is a room that will welcome you with open arms, however tiny it may be. Just as the people who make us happy tend to make us feel safe and secure, a room that makes us happy is easier to fall asleep in.

To be pleasing, the environment doesn't have to be pale or even relaxing. If you like red because it makes you feel strong, and feeling strong makes you feel safe, red might be the right color for your bedroom, even if the same color might make someone else too edgy to fall asleep. The bedroom doesn't have to be a cushiony or luxurious secret hideaway from the world—in fact, one psychologist has hypothesized that some people try to create cocoonlike bedrooms to compensate for the simple fact that they are not getting enough sleep. No matter the style or actual size of a bedroom, all it really has to do is make itself yours.

The purpose of this chapter is to prove that it is possible to create a bedroom you love—and that loves you back—no matter how little space you have. Yes, you can have an oversized bedstead. You can have a big comfortable chair, a chaise longue, even a separate sitting room. You can have an armoire, an antique desk, exercise equipment, a dressing room, storage space that makes life easy. As in the rest of life, you may not be able to have all of these in one room, but you will be able to have the ones that mean the most to you.

Sleep, Work, and Storage

This minuscule bedroom was almost too cramped for a decent-size bed and clothes storage, yet the couple also desperately needed room to accommodate the spillover from their living room library and a desk for work they occasionally brought home from the office.

Freestanding individual pieces would have made the room look like a mini-warehouse, so the solution was a sleek custom wall unit encompassing dressers, bookcases with adjustable shelves, and a double-duty desk/dressing table.

ABOVE: The wall unit was placed on a recessed plinth, and deliberately ends some eight inches short of the ceiling; the empty space keeps the eye from mistaking the unit for a wall that ends the room. Next to the desk, the dresser top holds a TV (not visible here). The fine lines of the open-frame chair make it almost invisible.

The decision was made to cover the structural column between the wall unit and the window in the same dark material as the rest of the walls to visually separate the pale oak wall unit and broaden the long, narrow room.

The contrast between the pale unit and the dark wall covering also draws the eye to the far corner and away from the center, where the bed and desk actually create the room's tightest passage. The dual-tone bed cover em-

phasizes the diagonal rather than the room's actual dimensions. Translucent glass shades on the bedside lamps let them glow like stars against the night sky. The low lamps and absence of headboard invite the eye to sweep across the room rather than move up and down, a motion that can make a room appear small.

The sisal carpet makes the floor seem an inch or so lower than it would have, had it been covered with a traditional pile carpet. The oak wall unit, the bed's open oak base, and the sisal carpet are bleached to remove yellow tones and let the surfaces recede into a "greige" background. For a couple on the run throughout the day and well into the evening, the room's spare Japanese style provides a welcome respite.

BED POTATOES

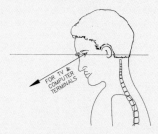

Looking at anything "eye level"—directly out from the center of the eye in a line almost perpendicular to the body—is comfortable only if our eye, head, and neck muscles are in motion, as they are when we walk down the street looking from side to side or when we are engaged in animated conversation. As long as those muscles are busy flexing and contracting, eye level is fine. But watching television or sitting at a computer requires the barest minimum of movement, and forcing the muscles to hold eyes, head, and neck still in an eye-level posture becomes tiring and eventually painful, and can even begin to put stress on the shoulders and back. The least stressful position, with the chin tilted down a bit and eyes looking down a bit, lets gravity do most of the work of keeping body parts in a healthy relationship.

As a rule of thumb, for watching TV in bed the bottom of the screen should be no lower than the top of the mattress. For those who watch while sitting up straight, the farther the TV is from the bed, the lower it can be. The farther you slip down into a reclining position, the higher the TV should be, but the top of the screen should never be higher than an imaginary line drawn straight out from your shoulder. If you prefer to watch while lying almost flat, the TV should be close to the ceiling and tilted toward you. There are devices available to hide the TV in the ceiling and pop it down only for viewing, but you need a large space above the ceiling to accommodate the set and the equipment. If you are most comfortable in a curled-up fetal position, you might want to place the TV to the side of the bed rather than at the foot, but if two people are in this position, one of them may block the other's view.

People who prefer to watch TV while using exercise equipment may have to do some extra calculations to find the best relationships among the TV, the bed, the exercise area, and the place where exercise equipment may be stored.

NEATNESS COUNTS

Neatness counts in the bedroom—at least the adult bedroom—more than in any other place in the house. Regardless of what the neighbors think of the rest of your home, it's the messy bedroom that will keep you awake at night, feeling you should get up and finish the report on the desk at the foot of the bed, finish putting away the clean laundry piled at the door, finish the dusting, finish the mending, finish all the chores that in your waking hours you realize can't fit into one day but that keep you tossing and turning when they are the last things you see before turning out the lights. (One exception: far from making you feel obliged to stay up reading, a bookcase has a noble quality that can be downright soothing.)

Find a graceful box to tuck the mending into; a beautiful scarf, an attractive tray, or even a big coffee-table book to place over the report; a basket for stashing the newspapers; and most important, closets and dressers so easy to get to that you actually want to put away your clothes, no matter how tired you are.

Create storage space for a hand-held mini-vac to pick up crumbs and other small messes you may find visually annoying at bedtime.

If the sight of exercise equipment makes you feel guilty, hide it behind a decorative screen. But keep in mind that if access to it is blocked, you may be discouraged from using it at all. Some equipment is manufactured to collapse and slide under a bed. A good solution is to buy the most attractive exercise equipment you can afford and tell yourself it is sculpture.

Two in the Space of One

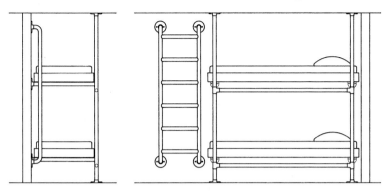

Section   Elevation

The two growing boys who share this bedroom insisted on "no decorating," but their parents were well aware that a great deal of "design" would be needed to accommodate beds, desks, dressers, exercise equipment, and horsing-around space for two kids in a room originally intended for only one.

ABOVE: A bunk bed made of painted two-inch industrial pipe bolted to the walls reduces physical bulk to the barest minimum. To keep the lines of the bed as open as possible, the matching ladder is attached to the wall. The five-inch-thick futon mattresses appear much thinner because they have been sunk into simple laminated box frames supported by the pipe scaffold. For younger children, additional pipe could be added to form a railing around the top bunk.

A custom-painted L-shaped wood desk/dresser provides an uninterrupted flow of work space and storage for two that invites the eye to sweep around two sides of the room. Repeating the black of the exercise equipment in the bunks and chairs also keeps the eye moving around the room. The art is hung somewhat above eye level in order to draw attention up and away from the boundary wall. Hanging the light track from long stems creates the illusion of an extra layer of air near the ceiling. The center of the room is deliberately kept clear in order to focus attention on the farthest distances.

A Big Look in a Small Space

The couple that slept here felt most secure among substantial furnishings and generous spaces, but their bedroom space seemed suited only to scaled-down pieces in tight arrangements. A circular bed seemed out of the question—but it began to solve the problem.

ABOVE: The ease of getting in and out of a circular bed—there are none of the implied rules associated with rectangular beds—more than makes up for the extra square inches of floor space a round bed takes up. In this room, the bed fits into the embrace of cabinetry that extends around three sides of the room. The linens and bedspread are custom made. Continuous neon light strips under the bed and dressers make them seem to float and give the illusion of a clear sweep of floor throughout the space. Horizontal bevel-edge mirror panels form a grid that gives the feeling of looking through a paned window into yet more space and makes the bed seem even farther away from the center of the room. The open-work light fixture contributes to the light, airy feeling. Mirroring the far closets also increases the sense of space.

A vanity with storage and TV cabinet overhead was built in the space that an inefficiently designed clothes closet took up. The vanity is installed on the diagonal; the foot room required is space that could not have been used for storage anyway.

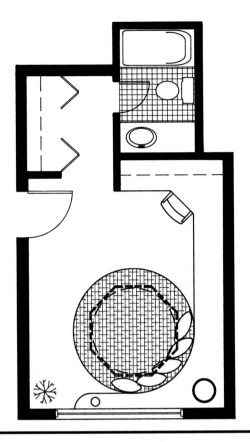

FOOL-THE-EYE TIPS

- Rid your bedroom of any objects that you truly dislike. If, for instance, you hate your bedspread, you will avoid looking at it and, in the process, miss seeing the space that extends beyond it too.
- You can accommodate large or overstuffed pieces of furniture in a small room as long as you place them as far as possible from the entry, and at an angle or to the side so the viewer doesn't see the furniture head on. Large pieces should be in a color that blends with the rest of the room—a pale armoire with pale walls and floor, a dark armoire with dark walls and floor. Use accent colors to bounce the eye around a large piece of furniture and distract from its mass.
- Lighting under beds and dressers seems to raise them and make the floor appear bigger.
- Mirrored walls give you the easiest view of yourself as well as multiplying the size of the room.
- Curve corners to make more generous passageways between pieces of furniture, to keep the eye moving in a smooth line, and to prevent bumps and bruises when you are in a hurry. (Allow a minimum of 30 inches between a bed and a dresser, and between the side of a bed and a wall.)

INTO THE CLOSET

To create more space, try extending the bedroom into the closet. Closets often take up twice as much physical space as they actually need for storage, because the space in front of them has to be kept free. Besides, experts now admit that hanging in closets puts a strain on clothes and shortens their lives, and recommend that, as much as possible, clothes be folded and stored in layers on flat surfaces. That means that almost everything you wear belongs in drawers or on shelves. Depending on the size and location of the closet (and what alternatives you have for the few coats, jackets, and dresses that must be on hangers), you can remove the door and hardware and insert a dresser or a desk/vanity with overhead cabinets, or even part of a bed. If the closet in a children's room abuts a wall, it is possible to slip about a third of a bunk bed into part of the closet and a desk and/or dresser into the remainder, leaving most of the room itself free for play.

KEEP EVERYTHING HANDY

Having to travel through the house to find things that you need in a bedroom can be a nuisance. Install a mini-refrigerator for nightcaps and cold drinks, milk for your morning coffee, even ice packs for sore muscles. A coffee maker can be used to make tea, herbal drinks, and hot chocolate. Incorporate space for at least one or two extra blankets in each bedroom so that no one has to prowl the halls on a cold night. Storage space is also needed for the heating pads, neck rolls, and under-the-knee wedges that everyone occasionally seems to need—and make sure there is a comfortably accessible outlet for any electrical heating pads; when you need one, crawling around under the bed to look for an outlet can aggravate the injury.

Greater than the Sum of Its Parts

The structural elements in this bedroom had created a tiny sleeping area and a disproportionately large (and nonfunctional) entry area. The challenge was to redesign the space to make the entry functional, and to allow three different but related areas—sleeping, dressing, and sitting—to flow into one another.

BELOW: The first step was to widen the entrance to the dressing room to connect it visually with the rest of the room. The bed remains in its cozy alcove-like area, while the entrance becomes a sitting room with a chaise longue built into a jog in the wall between two structural columns. Staining the built-in dressing-room cabinetry to match the color of the carpet allows the two surfaces to appear to be one larger surface. Stretching the large mirror the full height of the wall dissolves the ceiling line. The spare use of color lets selected objects—the vanity bench, the chaise, the antique desk—float airily in the otherwise monochrome space. The darker pediment over the door and a slim-trunked palm tree draw the eye upward and keep it from settling permanently on the bulk of the chaise. Frosted glass on the bedroom door lends an air of privacy as well as airiness.

Turning a Liability into an Asset

The owners of this apartment in the heart of a large city moved here when their children were grown, but they insisted on bringing a large, well-loved antique Chinese bedstead with them. The problem was how to fit the piece, and themselves, into a typical urban bedroom that was not much larger than the bed itself. The solution was to turn the bed's liabilities into assets by emphasizing—not hiding—its scale, allowing the entire room to function as a showcase for it.

ABOVE: Mirroring the entire wall opposite the foot of the bed doubled the bed's presence. Anything that might distract from the bed was cleared out, except for a few delicate pieces of the same style.

To compensate for the lack of dressers in the room, the bed's original base panels were removed and put into storage, and a high-end millwork shop with experience in antiques created storage drawers with touch-latch panels replicating the originals. If the bed ever goes on sale, the original panels can be restored with no loss in the value of the piece.

The horizontal line of the fine grass-cloth wall covering carries the eye quickly past the structural columns at the end of the room. The matching radiator cover/bookcase creates a framed view that pulls the eye through to the farthest distances.

Although a central focal point normally makes a room appear smaller, the bedcover's bold symbol helps emphasize the clear, open qualities of this room; the bedcover tucks in crisply and neatly around a five-inch futon.

Small Is Not Enough

The fact that babies are small and cribs are small doesn't mean that baby rooms will look large in comparison—in fact, as these parents learned almost immediately, the small scale of baby furniture can emphasize just how small the space really is.

ABOVE: The crib was pulled away from the wall and placed on a diagonal to give it a sense of importance in a room barely nine feet wide. The positioning at center stage also makes it possible for the largest number of doting visitors to gather around the crib. The choice of slatted rather than solid end pieces keeps the crib from seeming closed in.

The blue tint in the wall paint makes the room boundaries seem to recede, while the bright soft-textured wall hangings draw the eye around in a large sweep. The swagged valance lures the eye along a curved and therefore longer line as it moves from the window to the wall. The softly braided drapery at the side of the window helps to minimize the presence of the structural column in the corner. Dividing storage between two small dressers rather than placing everything in one large piece helps minimize bulk. The rattan chair lends an airy outdoor touch.

Cozy, but Open

Cozy patterns and lots of free-standing individual pieces of furniture are what make the owners of this traditional home feel comfortable and secure. But they also wanted their bedroom to seem as spacious as possible.

ABOVE: In a room filled with color and pattern, pale solid colors can become a focal point, drawing attention to areas that help visually enlarge a room. Here, the white in the wallcovering is picked up by the white open frame of the bed, the picture mat, and the somewhat larger than expected dresser-top vase, encouraging the eye to sweep around the room rather than settle on any of the large surfaces or busy patterns. Picking up the darker red or green from the wallpaper for use in focal points would have brought objects closer, and the walls with them. Keeping the pale accents at roughly the same level lets the eye move in a smooth expansive sweep on one plane.

The large rug reads almost like wall-to-wall carpet, with the placement of leggy furniture pieces half on the carpet and half on the wood floor blurring the sense of where the floor actually ends. The blue tone in the rug and the white paint above make both the floor and the ceiling recede.

The most unusual element in the room is the boldly colored tailored drapery at the window. Ruffles and pattern would have been more expected, but they would have closed the room up again and detracted from the space-enhancing view. Angling the bottom of the drapes lets in more view and draws the eye upward; hanging them directly from the ceiling gives the illusion that the window is full height.

Dividing to Get More

Although this bedroom started out as nothing more than a typical small modern box, it was transformed into the owners' ideal of a luxurious hotel suite, complete with a separate sitting room, a dressing room, free-standing traditional furniture, a four-poster king-size bed, and a filmy canopy.

ABOVE: Luckily, this couple recognized that a traditional canopy over the top of the bed would have obscured the bed's most striking aspect, the unusual finials that crown the four posts, and would also have made the ceiling appear lower. Instead, the desired canopy effect was achieved with the use of two sets of sheer full-length curtains spilling from rods installed at ceiling height across the full width of the space (ceiling-mounted supports at mid-rod prevent sagging). Closed, the curtains create three separate areas: an elegant sitting room at one end, a dressing room at the other, and, in the center, an intimate bedroom. Open, the curtains gather at the edges of the room and allude, in the manner of the theater, to more space in the wings. In addition to supporting the sheers, the rods add a sense of breadth to the room.

The same sheers are repeated at the window. To conserve space, the bulk of the sheers hangs close to the glass and stops at the top of the extended radiator cover; slim panels hang to the floor in front of the radiator to make sure the line is carried the full height of the room.

The strongest color in the room is used on the floor. Plush wine-colored wall-to-wall carpeting was chosen to help anchor the dark traditional wood furniture.

De-bulking the Furniture

The walls in this bedroom jog in and out in a way that doesn't leave much choice about furniture placement—there is no way to get the bed out of the center of the room. In addition, the room has 12-foot-high ceilings, which, far from ennobling a small room, just make the walls seem closer to one another. The transformation began with a light metal frame that gives the king-size bed some strength of character while drawing attention away from the mass of the mattress.

> ### AURAL SPACE
>
> Make sure your phone has a switch that can disable the ringer but still send calls to your answering machine. If you must keep a fax on all night, get a silent machine. If your computer beeps when it receives an electronic message, turn it off at bedtime and check for messages in the morning.

BELOW: A strong contrasting color in the bench draws attention away from the large mattress and lets the soft tones of the bedcover recede into the floor. To counteract the narrowing effect of the high ceiling, the light fixtures were located low on the wall. Walls were painted a pale green to help them recede, as well as to let the warmer carpet color take precedence. The massive slipper chair balances the bulk of the bed, but its upholstery, in the same color as the floor and the same value as the wall, is what allows it to blend in so well with its surroundings. Only a small throw pillow attracts attention.

In lieu of a standard night table, a custom-laminated piece with curved edges harmonizes with the other generously sized pieces in the room and doubles as a desk, accompanied by an open-frame metal chair. A ten-foot-long dresser on the far wall floats ten inches off the floor to let the floor flow right up to the wall. The folding screen in the corner conceals compact exercise equipment. The tree in the opposite corner is temporary until the couple finds the perfect armoire for the space. At that point, the bright green bench at the foot of the bed will fulfill its second function, as a visual divider marking off bed area and dressing area.

Bathrooms

Every now and then, a magazine or a book will feature bathrooms bigger than most living rooms—bathrooms that, in fact, contain sofas, armchairs, bookcases, beds, exercise equipment, and even fireplaces. But for most of us the bathroom continues to be the smallest room in the house, and the most frequently used as well. Given a choice, most of us would prefer *more* bathrooms to *bigger* bathrooms.

Unfortunately, adding bathrooms is a project prohibited by many local zoning authorities because they assume extra bathrooms mean extra people putting a strain on existing sewage systems. Even in large cities with elaborate sewage systems, adding a bathroom can be a hassle if you live in an apartment building—your room layout may not permit you to install a new toilet back to back with your existing fixtures, and you can be sure no one is going to agree to let you run new plumbing through all the apartments beneath you. Even if you plan only to hook into existing lines, you can count on at least some of your neighbors complaining about the strain on the plumbing system, even if your household size remains the same.

Smart space planning, however, can make any bathroom look bigger, serve more people, and contain more storage. A master bath, or even a children's bath, can be made to double as a powder room. Some functions can be moved so that, for instance, one person can shave inside the bathroom while another applies makeup at a stylish vanity right outside. Depending on the layout of your home, you may be able to turn a linen closet into a shower or wall off the toilet in a tiny room of its own, with a second door to another room or a hallway so that two people can use the same bathroom at the same time in complete privacy.

Even the space in a minimal five-foot-by-six-foot bathroom can be stretched with under-the-sink and over-the-toilet cabinetry (custom-made units will probably give you more storage space and door/shelf options than ready-made), storage carved out between the studs in the walls, and close attention to the color, lighting, and texture (see "Fool-the-Eye Tips" on page 73 and throughout this book).

An Opening Wedge

Near the public areas of the house, this master bathroom was ideally located to serve double duty as a powder room. The dilemma was how to create the space needed for a vanity table and tub-side table in a bathroom that already seemed too small.

RIGHT: A low, marble-topped, black-laminated chest fits snugly against the side of the tub (not visible here) to provide storage for bath accessories and a convenient surface for teacups, wineglasses, scented candles, books, reading glasses, and all the other aids to a luxurious bath. The plinth is recessed to lift the bulk of the chest to baseboard height and help draw the eye back to the wall.

The wedge shape of the vanity makes the area appear wider. Black drawers, a sleek black stool, and black wall-to-wall carpeting all seem to disappear beneath the vanity. The finely spattered paint treatment suggests a wall behind the wall.

The frosted sconce high on the wall casts a glow throughout the room, while also drawing attention to the vanity and away from the plumbing. The square lamp on the windowsill diffuses light evenly over facial planes during makeup sessions. The glass-block window provides security and privacy to this ground-floor bathroom, while its textured surfaces break up the distracting glare of early-morning sunlight.

GO BEYOND THE WALLS

Medicine cabinets are designed to fit the depth between interior walls, but there is no reason to limit yourself to the small sizes of off-the-shelf units. Every wall in your bathroom has behind it space roughly 6 inches deep and 14 inches wide that you can recoup for storage of cosmetics, grooming and bath accessories, cleaning preparations, and the like. There's even space back there to insert shelves to hold scented candles, a bottle of wine or brandy, some nice glasses, a small tape player, and maybe even a tiny coil to heat water and some packets of herbal teas.

You may be able to recoup deeper space from behind a wall that hides plumbing pipes or ventilation ducts. Remove the medicine cabinet or a piece of baseboard in an adjacent room, and poke around with a flashlight and a ruler to find out how much available space is in there.

Found Space

The couple who owned this home wanted a luxurious master bathroom with a double-basin vanity that would eliminate the jostling for sink space first thing in the morning. What they had was a square bathroom—entered by a circuitous route that wound through a dressing room—with the regulation bathtub, toilet, and single sink and a tremendous amount of wasted floor space dictated by plumbing lines, a window, and a door.

The old doorway to the dressing room was sealed with drywall, a new one was created to line up with the entry to the bathroom, and the clothes closet was switched into the bedroom (see before-and-after floor plans).

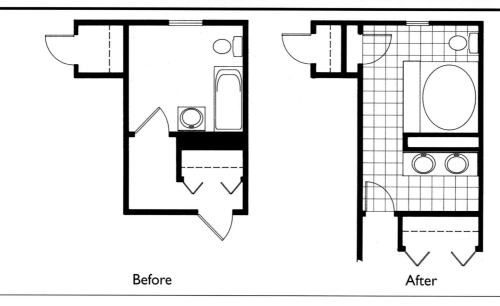

Before   After

Every bathroom needs at least one mirror for shaving and makeup application, but don't stop there. Move the medicine cabinet to a side wall or buy one that fits in a corner, and mirror every inch of the sink wall; the more area that is mirrored, the larger the room will appear.

For the best facial illumination, lighting should be placed along both sides and above the mirror; second best is along the sides; third is a strip above the mirror. The worst alternative is a single light bulb above the mirror.

For additional information on the use of reflective illusions, see "Walls." To help keep the mirrors from clouding up (and the rest of the room from developing mildew), talk to an architect or a contractor about your ventilation needs.

LEFT: With the old closet ripped out, the dressing room now had space for a double-basin vanity on the wall that contains the original plumbing lines. To create ambiguous boundaries, terrazzo was used to cover the bathroom floor, walls to wainscot height, and the vanity top; the upper walls have linen-textured vinyl in a similar shade. The vanity mirror reflects a mirrored shelf unit installed between the studs in the back wall of the new clothes closet. The color of the laminate cabinetry accents the edges of the two medicine chests, making them appear to float on the mirrored wall, and then bounces the eye through the lavatory to the far end of the bath, where it reappears in the venetian blinds.

RIGHT: A new tub, with a wide surround for sitting and for holding bath accessories, makes better use of the floor space in the original bathroom area. "Found space" between the wall studs is used to house touch-latch cabinets and open shelves within the mirrored walls surrounding the tub. Brass handrails on the terrazzo backsplash provide safety as well as a luxurious golden shine. In the opposite corner, seen in the reflection, a shallow linen closet was carved from the back of the adjacent room's clothes closet. Framed art in compatible colors lends interest to the opposite wall without appearing to break it up into small sections. Recessed downlights for an even allover glow are centered in each of the large mirrored ceiling tiles.

Clear Views

In this house one of the bathrooms was very convenient, midway between the back door and the main living areas, and tended to get a lot of use because of its location. The owners wanted it to do triple duty: as an everyday bathroom for the children, as a powder room serving both living room and family room, and as a clean-up station for family members who entered covered with beach sand or mud.

- See-through enclosures or curtains—or none at all—keep the tub or shower within the visually accessible space of the room.
- Under-rim sinks are more expensive because of the labor involved to achieve a perfectly fitting vanity top, but may be the best choice in a too-small bathroom; their longer, unbroken line makes the vanity appear more generous.
- Regrouting wall tile in a contrasting color creates a lattice-work effect that gives the illusion that the real wall is just beyond. If you have broken tiles, remove them and install contrasting or decorative replacements. (You also can break and remove some deliberately to create a pattern of old and new tiles.)
- If you stick with white fixtures, you can use any other color you want in the rest of the room—even a bold or deep color for the walls and the floor of a tiny bathroom. The eye will always go to the white fixtures, which, in a bathroom, tend to be arranged around the perimeter.
- If you invest in a beautiful sink, use a single downlight to make it a focal point, but augment it with softer strips along or above the mirror to avoid casting shadows on your face.
- Decorative faucets can create the illusion of space by drawing attention toward the farthest edges of the bathroom.
- Luxury comes cheaper in the bathroom than anywhere else in the house. For instance, for the same price as a marble or fancy tile living room floor, you probably can cover the floor, walls, and ceiling of the average bathroom in the same material or in solid surfacing that shows no seams and comes, at least in the lighter colors, with matching basins.

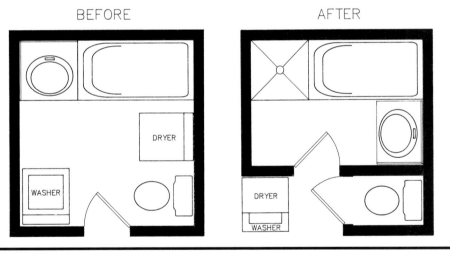

BEFORE

AFTER

FACING PAGE: Reflected in the mirror is the most important design element, a clear acrylic shower stall that permits views straight through to the farthest corner; an opaque wall separating the tub and the shower would have foreshortened the room considerably.

The shower is sited in a space formerly occupied by the sink, which is now in the original toilet location; the toilet was moved somewhat to the right and given its own niche with a separate door (not visible here). The extra space—basically the width of the toilet and the length of the bathroom—was originally a laundry area, with appliances and sorting surfaces arranged in a row; it became available when the dryer was wall mounted over the washer (see

plan) in a closet accessible from outside the bathroom, and a rolling kitchen counter was put into use for sorting.

The bathroom surfaces require only a quick wipe to make them presentable to guests. The plastic-laminated vanity and the non-skid ceramic floor and textured tile tub surround are a pale gray that gives prominence to the white fixtures and high-gloss wall tiles. Attaching the towel rack to the end of the vanity lets the wall space continue unbroken around the tub and shower stall. A vanity-width mirror doubles the space visually. A laminated medicine chest (not visible here) is attached above child height on the near wall and contains items that adult guests might need. Gleaming faucets provide a note of luxury.

The Cosmetics Corner

Because neither bedroom nor bathroom was large enough to permit two people to get themselves ready for work at the same time, the business couple that lives here began every day grimly trying to avoid each other as they groomed themselves. If the wife stored her cosmetics in the bathroom, it seemed the husband was always in there shaving just when she needed them; if she used them in the bedroom, he had to squeeze himself into a corner to get dressed. When either one of them tried to shave or put on makeup at the kitchen sink, the other one invariably needed the space to begin making breakfast. Compounding the problem was a shallow linen closet next to the bathroom; the closet was not really needed and was taking up valuable space.

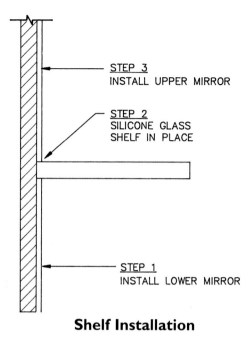

STEP 3
INSTALL UPPER MIRROR

STEP 2
SILICONE GLASS
SHELF IN PLACE

STEP 1
INSTALL LOWER MIRROR

Shelf Installation

OTHER SPACE SOURCES

- Get medicine and first-aid supplies out of the medicine cabinet and put them someplace where they can be reached quickly—a kitchen cabinet, for instance—without disturbing others who might be using the bathroom. This tactic will also free up the medicine chest for bath and grooming accessories. (Keep some aspirin or other over-the-counter pain remedies in the bathroom, however, since that's where guests expect to find them.)
- To make a sauna do double duty, install a shower head on the wall.
- In a truly tiny bathroom, cover all the surfaces with tile, slope the floor gently toward a drain, and turn the entire room—toilet, sink, and all—into a walk-in shower, the way they do in Europe. As you might imagine, the shower will splash water all over the room, but for some households this may be the only way to gain an extra shower.

FACING PAGE: The linen closet door and shelves were removed to create a vanity niche, which, along with the rest of the dark, narrow hall, was covered with floor-to-ceiling mirrors to create a sense of endless space. A glass shelf was inserted into the niche for use when the wife is applying cosmetics, but all her grooming equipment is actually stored under the lift-up needlepoint cushion on the stool. The shelf, bracketless, was set on the lower segments of the wall mirrors, and the upper segments installed last. The existing hall floor was stripped and stained a pink shade that eases the transition to the bathroom. The husband's shaving equipment is stored in a medicine chest on the side wall inside the bathroom, so that the entire wall over the sink and toilet could be mirrored; the mirrors almost double the sense of space. A grille-covered downlight strip provides a continuous horizontal glow, reinforcing the clean swath of mirror. Where under-sink storage cabinets would have cut off the flow of the floor, a pedestal sink, matched to the toilet, lets the eye penetrate all the way to the back wall. A bath rug was chosen to allow the tile color to sweep up the wall in one long flow; wall-to-wall carpet in purple would have called too much attention to itself and the joint between wall and floor. A reflection over the vanity shelf in the hall shows the swagged shower curtain rising all the way to the ceiling to draw the eye diagonally along one of the longest lines in the bathroom. In order for the husband to exit the bathroom comfortably without tripping over his wife, the bathroom door was extended the full width of the hall.

Kitchens

The kitchen is the heart of the house, possibly because, from birth, we find the people we know and trust spending a lot of time there. At a party for forty adults, twenty of them will try to squeeze themselves into the kitchen, most not even looking for food or drink; they will be there because they know that's where the action is. More than one host has had the experience of turning off the kitchen lights and leaving, only to return to a heated political or sports discussion taking place in complete darkness. Even animals gravitate toward the kitchen, and, again, not for the food; they want the warmth.

As a result, most of us keep trying to enlarge our kitchens even though the act of cooking doesn't really require much space—a sink, stove, refrigerator, and counter all located close enough together to minimize walking. In fact, from a purely functional point of view, the ideal should be a kitchen so small that a cook need only turn around to reach everything; see the sidebar "The Work Triangle" (page 77).

But human beings want more than function. They want one another, they want attractive surroundings, and they don't want to be confined. If function meant giving up the other things we want, most of us would seriously consider sacrificing function. But we don't have to. Careful planning can result in efficient kitchens that also please the eye and warm the heart.

Careful kitchen planning is also crucial because redesign tends to be costly. Interestingly, the kitchen is usually the least frequently redesigned room, not because of cost, but because its appliances and materials are so durable—according to the National Association of Home Builders, an electric range lasts about seventeen years, laminates up to fifteen years, cabinets fifteen to twenty years, granite more than twenty years, sinks and vinyl tile up to thirty years, ceramic tile just about forever. Since you'll probably be living with your kitchen design for a long time, put in some extra effort now to get it just right.

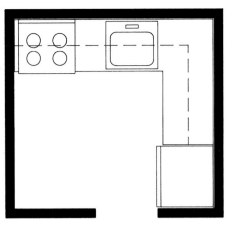

THE WORK TRIANGLE

For the greatest convenience and least fatigue, most interior designers who specialize in nothing but kitchens recommend that the major appliances be arranged in the form of a triangle that reflects how the job of cooking is done. The legs of the triangle do *not* correspond to the walls but to the path between the major appliances, which may or may not parallel the walls (see diagrams). No matter how large the room, the three sides of the triangle should not total more than 22 feet. Most important, since the triangle is where hot surfaces, sharp tools, and electrical appliances are located, it should not be on traffic routes used by people—or pets—to get to and from other parts of the house.

Since meal preparation seems to take us most often from the sink to the refrigerator and from the sink to the stove, the sink should be the central point of the triangle, with the stove on one side, the refrigerator on the other. This arrangement also keeps the heat generated by the stove from driving up the refrigerator's energy requirements. The three appliances should be separated by countertops at least 24 inches wide—the minimum width for getting any work done.

Since right-handed people tend to prefer a dish drainer to the right of the sink, their stoves should be placed to the left; they will also find a dishwasher to the right of the sink and pot racks to the right of the stove the most convenient arrangement. Left-handed people should reverse the arrangement. (Where the cook and the person in charge of cleanup don't share the same handedness, victory goes to the cook, who otherwise will constantly be trailing pots back and forth above the dish drainer or, equally inconveniently, relying on his or her weakest arm to move heavy objects.) If two cooks regularly work together, or you expect guests to pitch in, try to set up a second triangle—say, an island with a second sink that forms a new triangle with the existing stove and refrigerator.

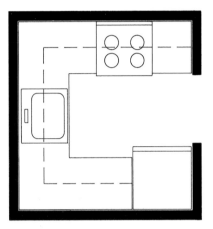

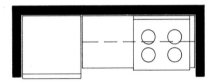

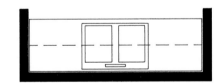

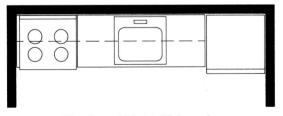

Kitchen Work Triangles

A Better Outlook

This kitchen belongs to a man who loves to cook, especially when he has crowds of friends keeping him company. It bothered him that in the original kitchen the appliances were strung out along one wall so that he had to cook with his back to his guests, creating a distinctly antisocial situation. The installation of a center island with a second sink and additional work surface let the cook face outward. At the same time, the heat-generating cooktop and ovens were kept back against the wall.

SIZING UP THE EQUIPMENT

No matter how specifically adapted to individual needs or peculiar space constraints, all kitchens tend to be made up of standard parts with standard measurements. When sketching out your dream kitchen, keep in mind the following dimensions:

- The smallest practical kitchen sink is 6 inches deep and 16 inches wide, and requires at least 12 inches of side clearance, mainly to accommodate elbows, from an abutting wall or appliance.
- Dishwashers are typically 24 inches wide; some are made to fit under the sink, without the need to move plumbing, but the awkward stretch to scrape and rinse in the sink could possibly put a strain on your back (and discourage younger dishwashers altogether).
- Full stoves tend to be 30 inches wide; narrower ones are available, but don't count on their ovens to hold holiday turkeys. Look for ovens that double as broilers.
- Drop-in stove tops range from 24 inches wide for tight four-burner arrangements to 36 inches wide for models that incorporate grills in the middle; again, count on at least 12 inches of clearance from the next wall or appliance.
- Standard single-door refrigerators run from 30 to 36 inches wide, plus a half inch of maneuvering room on each side. Allow 2 to 3 inches of ventilating space between the refrigerator and any upper cabinets; heat rises, and if you block the upper portions of the ventilation spaces, your refrigerator will have to work harder and use more electricity. To avoid tearing into floors or ceilings to insert water lines, refrigerators that dispense ice or ice water should be located near the kitchen sink or should back up on a bathroom. Some refrigerators are now available to fit flush with a standard kitchen counter rather than jut a few inches farther into the room.
- In an eat-in kitchen, try not to let the cook's traffic paths overlap the 24 inches of free space needed for pushing chairs in and out.
- Kitchen pass-throughs should be 36 or 42 inches above floor level to avoid exposing kitchen clutter and mess. If the pass-through is also a dining counter, use a 24-inch stool for a 36-inch-high surface, or a 30-inch stool for a 42-inch-high surface. Opening up space between upper cabinets and ceiling increases the sense of airiness (and may be enough to satisfy local building-code requirements for ventilation in windowless kitchens).

FACING PAGE: In a room whose far surfaces are covered in a recessive, space-expanding white, the dark, shiny work surface of the island seems to float and create a sense of indeterminate space around it. A black dropped ceiling soffit contains storage accessible from the kitchen side and a custom light fixture of shiny metal. The far end of the work surface (seen in reflection) cantilevers out to double as a small dining space, with 15 inches of knee room and storage for stools underneath. The rounded corners of the island create a long visual line and protection against bruises.

All the work surfaces, both black and white, are synthetic solids with unifying inlaid metal bands. Fluorescent tubes and a pull-down exhaust hood for the range/grill are hidden under the full-height cabinets. The cabinets have no visible hardware to break up the smooth line along the back wall. The mirrored full-height backsplashes give a visual lift to the upper cabinets and window and also make the wall appear farther away than it really is. The small open shelf over the sink provides a nicely humid spot for plants.

CABINET FITTINGS

Kitchen cabinet specialty shops can supply you with cabinet fittings that make maximum use of your storage space. These include bins; rolling shelves; vertical holders for lids, platters, trays, and cutting boards; carousels for upper and lower corner cabinets; and waterproof tilt-out drawers to hold soap and scrubbers in the sliver of waste space in front of the sink. You can start out with a few and gradually upgrade over time.

If you plan to use existing cabinets, these specialty fittings may still make better use of your space than those available in housewares stores.

Playing the Angles

At first glance the kitchen in this house seemed to be a good size and ideally located next to the family room. It was only after the household moved in that it discovered that the door to the garage and the door to the dining room (and the rest of the house) had created a traffic lane that severely restricted the places a free-standing kitchen table could be placed. The solution was to design a new eating area that would extend out from the cabinets at an angle that avoided the traffic route.

ABOVE: The new kitchen table juts out at an angle from the cabinets, leaving the path between the two doors free and permitting direct access to the refrigerator from the family room. A pass-through and two-way see-through storage cabinet with glass shelves helps to maintain the visual openness of the room. The lower shelf that connects to the table is a convenient depot for last-minute morning items like keys, lunch bags, schoolbooks, and attaché cases; in a pinch, an extra diner can be squeezed in there.

The dining table, all the kitchen work surfaces, and the full-height backsplashes are covered in the same laminate. This creates the illusion of an expanding horizontal plane as well as of a greater height between upper and lower cabinets. Similar floor and cabinetry tones were chosen for the same reason, to blur the boundaries between surfaces and allow them to flow into one another. The wooden trim on the work surfaces reinforces the horizontal line; its bullnose shape softens the edges. A wood baseboard seems to extend the floor into the pass-through unit.

The work triangle extends along the walls, confining cooking activities to the rear and leaving the central area open. "Spaghetti chairs"—seats and backs are made of clear plastic strands on pared-down frames—keep the dining area uncluttered and offer the least distraction from the long, flowing lines of the room.

Free the Prisoners of the Kitchen

This home attracted a couple that had one worry about it: they felt the walls of the tiny, windowless kitchen would quickly begin to close in on them. They were especially concerned that the room would make them feel like virtual prisoners when they were cooking for guests. They liked the idea of removing the wall between the kitchen and the dining room, but feared that they weren't neat enough to let their cooking area be on such public view.

BELOW: Worries about neatness disappeared with the installation of cabinets with fully fitted interiors that make putting things away a quick and easy habit, and free the kitchen from space-gobbling clutter. Built-in carousels keep the corner cabinets fully usable, while the work surface corners become display areas for attractive serving pieces.

An elegant but serviceable palette of granite and fruitwood was chosen to let the objects in the room, rather than its spatial limits, become the center of attention; instead of fixing on solid surfaces the eye bounces around from sink to cooktop to chrome hardware to the window-like display cabinet that forms a focal point above eye level in the middle of the back wall. In the process, the eye ignores the split between the under-sink cabinets and the dishwasher below.

A range hood concealed in the upper cabinet pulls down and out when needed. The floor pattern follows the boxy form of the room and keeps the eye moving back toward the glass-front display cabinet.

CABINETS

- Standard upper cabinets are 12 inches deep; lower cabinets are 24 inches deep. Countertops are generally 25 or 26 inches deep.
- Most ready-made cabinet doors come in widths from 12 inches to 18 inches; doors wider than 18 inches require expensive, heavy-duty hinges.
- Standard counters are 36 inches high, but they can be raised or lowered to suit the needs of your particular household; generally, counters should be 2 inches below the cook's elbow. If you are raising the counters, make sure to adjust the height of the upper cabinets proportionately. If the counters will be used for dining, make sure your chair seats are 12 inches below the counter.
- Counters where people will eat or will work sitting down require at least 15 inches of depth underneath for knee space and stool storage.
- Lower cabinets need a toe-room plinth about $2^{1}/_{2}$ inches high and should be recessed 3 inches; you may want to talk to a custom kitchen cabinet shop about installing shallow drawers with recessed handles in the empty plinth.
- The space between upper and lower cabinets is usually 15 to 18 inches high. The most common height for a backsplash is 4 inches, but for a very sleek look, a 2-inch backsplash can be used as long as the wall above it is completely covered with a very durable washable material, such as plastic laminate, polished stone, ceramic tile, vinyl wall covering, metal, mirror, or solid surface counter material.
- A standard upper cabinet is 27 inches high, but a custom shop can help you obtain cabinets that go all the way up to the ceiling, giving you up to one third more storage and the illusion of a higher ceiling. The cabinets should be installed as tight to the ceiling as possible—the cabinetmaker or custom shop should allow a little extra material to be shaped during installation if the ceiling turns out to be wavy or slanted; the doors should line up with themselves rather than with the base cabinet or the ceiling.
- A lip of 2 inches at the lower edge of the upper cabinets is enough to conceal fluorescent fixtures that shine on countertops. For maximum concealment, place the fixtures toward the front of the cabinet. Make sure you have adequate ambient light to see into upper cabinets as well as to prevent the momentary blindness that can result when focus shifts from a brightly lit surface to dark surroundings. Make sure ambient lighting fixtures don't interfere with the swing of cabinet doors.
- Make sure that when cabinet and appliance doors swing open they don't interfere with people using the stove or sink.
- Fit corner cabinets—upper and lower—with carousels to make storage and retrieval as efficient as possible.
- Counter corners may not be too useful for food preparation but they work well for open storage and display: coffee pot, blender, food processor, juicer, toasters, electric frying pan, cookbooks, canisters, knife rack, tool collections, dish drainer, a beautiful bread box, liquor collection, or decorative serving pieces. Remember to include extra electrical outlets in these areas. Diagonal cabinets are available, but they tend to eat up visual space. A sink may be placed in a counter corner, but not a stove top, because of the temptation to reach over the burners to get to items stored in the back wedge of the countertop.
- Plan on storing your most frequently used food, tools, and equipment between knee and shoulder height.
- Good cooks will tell you that spice racks are not the best place to store herbs and spices, which belong in a dark, cool place. A kitchen drawer is better and just as convenient; when the drawer is opened, wonderful scents will waft into the room.

FOOL-THE-EYE TIPS

- A backsplash that matches the counter and extends all the way up the wall to the upper cabinets creates the most spacious look, as long as you choose a cool color that will not make the backsplash surface seem to pull forward.
- Mirrored backsplashes create the greatest sense of space and are easily brightened with a grease-cutting glass cleaner (which is also a good cleaner for enameled surfaces). Clear silicon caulk is the best for waterproofing the joint between the counter and the mirror.
- A range hood that collapses back into the cabinetry when not in use will shave six inches of storage off the upper cabinet, but the trade-off is worth the extra physical and visual space that becomes available when there is no heavy-duty cooking going on.

- Hanging plants take up no floor space but draw the eye upward. Since heat and gases collect near the ceiling, look for tenacious plants like philodendron and grape ivy.
- Diagonal or diamond-patterned floors draw attention away from eye level and along the longest lines in the room.
- A double sink will make it possible for you to hide—and soak—dirty dishes in one tub, while leaving the other free; the cover of the soaking tub can be used as a work surface.
- Kitchen cabinet doors can often open into the dining area to hold everything needed for setting the table, and keep helpers from getting in the way of the cooks (see drawings).

Cabinetry Shared by Kitchen and Dining Room

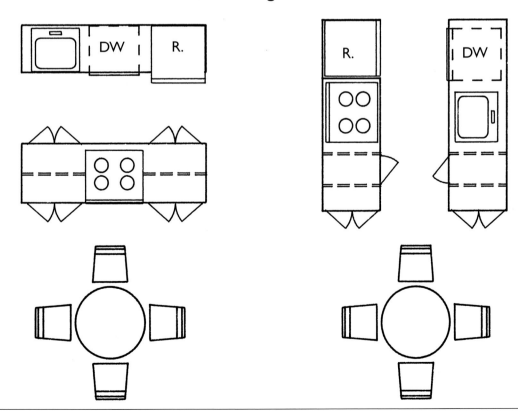

Expanding the Shrunken Kitchen

This older home had a good-sized kitchen, but when the owners decided to add a much-needed first-floor bathroom, utilizing the same plumbing lines, the kitchen inevitably shrunk in size. But only temporarily; when the kitchen was renovated, its sleek, streamlined design made it appear much larger.

WORK-SURFACE MATERIALS

A slab of stone and a slab of the synthetic solid surface material that mimics stone cost about the same to buy and install, but solid surfaces have several advantages: they can be joined seamlessly to turn corners or sweep into backsplashes, scratches are easily removed, some have matching sinks, and carving and inlays are less expensive than in stone. Plastic laminates cost less than half the price of plain stone or solid surfacing; special edging and inlays cost about half too. Laminates come in the widest variety of colors, patterns, and even textures of all surface materials.

Marble stains easily and is hard to clean, making it a poor choice for any kitchen surface—but a slab of marble that will fit in your freezer is still the ideal surface for rolling pastry dough. Wood blocks have to be kept scrupulously clean with bleach and wire brushes in order to avoid the growth of unfriendly bacteria; attractive plastic cutting boards are a much better idea. Wood trim needs a few extra coats of polyurethane and a few renewing coats every two or three years.

KITCHEN AIDS

There are several sources of kitchen components:

- Department stores and discount outlets sell ready-made cabinetry and even large appliances.
- Custom cabinetry shops can make cabinets from scratch; many have interior design services to help with some design details, such as working out symmetrical arrangements in oddly shaped spaces.
- High-end kitchen design shops sell mass-produced domestic and imported cabinets that can be customized to your needs; some offer design services.
- Some designers specialize only in kitchens. The initials CKD (Certified Kitchen Designer) after their names means they have been tested by the National Kitchen and Bath Association.

Since the kitchen takes a lot of hard use but tends to last a long time because of its durable materials and finishes, this is the one room where you might want to consider splurging on a professional designer.

FACING PAGE: Extra-height cabinets provide maximum storage space. Covered in a space-expanding white laminate, the cabinets make the ceiling appear higher. The use of one color for cabinets, ceiling, and floor lets the three surfaces flow into one another, while occasional splashes of black keep the eye moving.

Full-height mirrored backsplashes on abutting walls not only lift the upper cabinets but create reflections of reflections, suggesting infinite space—and more windows—beyond. A decorative brass rail creates a long unifying line around the work surfaces and doubles as a rack for towels, pot holders, aprons, and even curve-handled utensils. The raised-panel doors ,and the brass rail and round brass doorknobs—all sealed to prevent discoloration—not only keep the eye traveling but are traditional notes in an otherwise sleek kitchen.

Too Big, But Not Big Enough

This kitchen was just big enough to create some problems but, it seemed, not big enough to solve any of them. All the work surfaces and appliances were stretched out along the walls, creating a work triangle whose legs were too long and which required too much walking during complex meal preparations. At the same time, there was a gap in the middle of the room that suggested an eat-in kitchen but was really too small for a table and chairs. The solution was to utilize the center space for a cooking island instead. The island cuts down considerably on walking—the sink, in fact, can be reached just by turning around—and provides a lot of new storage, since the cooktop is only 6 inches deep.

BELOW: On the sides of the island, away from traffic, a 15-inch collar of dining space was installed at table height—29 inches off the floor—making it possible to use ordinary chairs rather than high stools. The children use this surface for homework when the cooktop is not in use. The dual height of the island also serves a visual function by making the island look less massive.

All the vertical surfaces are covered with the same recessive white laminate, with white hardware to visually push back the boundaries of the room. A collection of bright canisters and attractively packaged groceries draws the eye to a corner of full-height mirrored backsplashes. Some extra investment went into a refrigerator that fits flush to the counter instead of jutting into the room a few inches, as most do.

Spare Rooms

An entire extra room is cause for rejoicing, but unfortunately, too many people wind up, almost by accident, using it for storage rather than for living. They keep tossing in boxes and out-of-season clothes, all the while telling themselves it's the spare room, but it isn't; it's the junk room.

A storage room is not always the luxury it seems, either. It is usually so unsightly that it has to be closed off during parties, and it takes a frantic nerve-wracking push to turn it into a bedroom for an overnight guest.

In a world where extra rooms are increasingly scarce, it's an extravagant waste to go on using one for haphazard storage. Every household has at least one member who needs a quiet place—to concentrate on finances, read serious books and magazine articles, work on projects brought home from the office, or exercise in privacy—far more than he or she needs a storage room. Every household also needs a neutral space where members can retreat to cool off during an argument. And everyone, even a person who lives alone, needs to be able to run away from home without having to leave the house.

Spare rooms are rarely perfect spaces. They tend to be small and are often disproportionately narrow. If there is a room with strange angles or fussy little corners, too many doors (all inconveniently located), or structural columns that break up the space at ex-actly the wrong points—this is the room that will wind up as the spare room.

Traditionally, spare rooms also have tended to appear as children grow up and move away; at this point the family room or, alternatively, the living room may become a spare room too. And as more and more people relax in easy chairs with one-dish meals or take-out food, dining ells and breakfast nooks also have begun to take on a spare room aspect—all most would need is a partition and door. Older homes may have maid's rooms of the dimensions and shapes that explain why it has always been "so difficult to get good help." While no one should have to live in such places, they may make perfect small home offices, dens, meditation rooms, or short-term guest quarters. (If your home business requires you to work with chemicals—such as commercial art sprays—don't ask guests to eat or sleep in this room. You yourself probably shouldn't do any kind of aerobic exercise in it either.)

No one says you have to pretend to lead the life some housing developer planned for you. A formal living room or dining room that is used only on major holidays may be, in reality, a spare room. An old-fashioned Murphy bed in a beautiful armoire could turn the living room into an extraordinary suite for overnight guests. Alternatively, single beds (36 inches wide) with interesting frames and wonderful throw pillows can do double duty as supplementary seating for formal entertaining, as well as comfortable beds when the room becomes the guest suite. A seldom-used living room can also become the most elegant of offices as long as the business furnishings and equipment complement the style and quality of your original living room furniture; there also needs to be a way to whisk your work materials out of sight when company comes.

In some family mythologies, the unexpected guest winds up sleeping on the dining room table, but even with armoire-contained Murphy beds or elegant day beds, there really is no way to convince a guest that a dining room is anything but a dining room. On the other hand, the rarely used dining room is *the* obvious place to run a home business; see the sidebar "Is Your Dining Room Really the Spare Room?" below for suggestions on using it for both purposes.

Because a well-planned spare room tends to have multiple uses, the ideas in the following examples could be used equally well for studio apartments.

IS YOUR DINING ROOM REALLY THE SPARE ROOM?

If you use your dining room only once or twice a year, it may be wise to consider it an office or den from the outset, one that just happens to convert quickly into a gracious dining room on grand occasions. A book-lined room generally has a formal air, and filing and other storage cabinets can double as buffets and serving stations.

Since the room will still have a formal function (and since your work deserves just as nice a setting as your meals do), invest in custom cabinetry, custom adaptation of your existing dining room cabinetry to accommodate file drawers, or executive office furnishings. (Newspapers often carry advertisements for warehouse sales of designer-quality office furniture.)

In a bookcase-over-storage-cabinet arrangement, remove the bottom shelf of the bookcase and rest the uprights directly on the storage cabinets so you have a clear, level surface from the front of the cabinet to the back for use as a buffet or serving station. Make sure you attach the bookcase firmly to the wall and resist the temptation to use the clear space for any permanent office equipment—you don't want to have to relocate a computer or a whole shelf of reference books five minutes before your dinner guests arrive. If you always keep your active files in a drawer, you won't have to waste time trying to hide them when your office turns into a dining room.

Keep all the office equipment that looks out of place at dinner parties—computers, fax machines, printers, modems, drafting tables, copiers, answering machines, and the like—on wheels to scoot them out of sight in a flash. Most of this equipment shouldn't be around food or drink anyway (although you can safely fold up a laptop computer and slip it into a bookcase).

If your work does not require the continual use of large surfaces, you might want a shelf desk that collapses back into the cabinetry when not in use. If your desk is larger but on wheels, you won't even have to clear off the top when company comes—just throw a towel over it and roll it away.

For jobs that require sizable surfaces, you might as well use the dining table—very few office jobs pose as much danger to a good table as eating on it does—with, if necessary, wheeled file cabinets slipped underneath. If it is too complicated to file your working materials away for a party and set them up again in the right order the next morning, lay them out on a collapsible trolley, cover them with a towel, and roll them away. If you have an attractive shelved tea trolley and a beautiful scarf, your equipment may not even have to leave the room.

Three in One

This narrow room is so tiny it was on the verge of disappearing, but some visual tricks and some clever —and economical—storage turned it into a combination body-building workshop/jazz center/guest room.

ABOVE: Mirroring one wall from floor to ceiling creates an upscale health-spa atmosphere while doubling the perceived space—more than doubling it, actually, since the mirrors also reflect the outdoor space and light brought into the room through the windows. Setting a good-looking, compact set of stationary body-building equipment along the mirrored wall highlights its sculptural quality and reinforces the spa look of the room.

Along the opposite wall is a smooth, uncluttered sweep of storage wall, assembled from store-bought units finished in bleached oak and containing a Murphy bed. The unit holds the jazz collection and stereo equipment, along with books, out-of-season clothes, and a television set that can be watched through the mirror by a guest propped up on the opened bed. Back-lit cut-out niches (reflected in the mirror) add a sense of depth. A column of round-edge bookshelves creates a smooth ending for the storage wall.

Under the window, a simple laminated radiator cover creates the totally false impression that there are more books and records, rather than a radiator, behind it. A Roman shade ensures complete privacy during exercise sessions or when guests are sleeping. Lush carpeting, generously scaled seating, and a modest display of art lend an expansive touch of luxury.

Home Theater

Home theater equipment is simply too attention-grabbing for most living rooms or family rooms, but the spatial requirements—any large viewing screen should be roughly 12 feet away from the viewer and out of the line of general room lighting—can make it a tight fit in a spare room.

This small, narrow room was the only one a movie-loving family had available for a home theater. Unfortunately, inconveniently placed doors and angled windows made two of the walls unsuitable for seating or screen; the available walls were just barely far enough apart to work. So every inch had to be used as efficiently as possible.

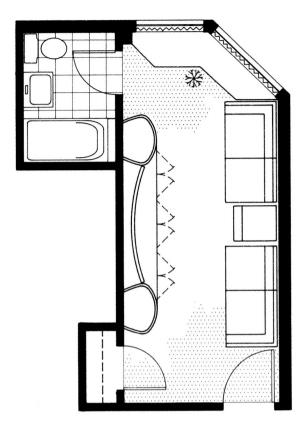

The curved wings of a custom-built wall unit shade the screen from general room lighting while also smoothing entrances and exits through the immediately adjacent doors. The base cabinet provides plenty of storage for the family's extensive videotape collection, along with amplifiers, tape deck, CD player, turntable, speakers, television, and record, cassette, and CD collections. When these entertainment sections are opened, their doors disappear into side pockets. The bottom of the unit is recessed to prevent the eye from assuming that the unit—rather than the wall well behind it—is the boundary of the room. The projector for the large-screen TV is tucked between parts of a custom-made sectional sofa.

The subdued monochrome color scheme adds a feeling of spaciousness to the small room and prevents any visual "noise" from distracting viewers. Dimmer controls adjust the indirect light that glows behind, above, and below the wall unit to comfortable viewing levels. At the window, black 3-inch vertical blinds cut the glare that can make even the best picture appear faded; white blinds would have allowed light to leak into the room. Bookcases under the windows let the room double as a mini-library and display center for art objects; a wide-angled cut near the door permits easy passage to and from the bathroom.

FOOL-THE-EYE TIPS

- Squared-off corners on furnishings and wall units can create a hemmed-in feeling and, in tight quarters, a potential for bruises. Curves eliminate this problem and create a feeling of expansiveness and space.
- Filling a wall with pictures can make it seem more important and therefore larger. Sculpture, on the other hand, has the ability to carve out illusionary space around it, but should be used sparingly. While one or two pieces of sculpture can create a feeling of space, more than that can create a visual turf war.
- With their long slender legs, horse sculptures create an especially airy feeling (but don't run out to buy one unless you really appreciate this type of sculpture).
- Office-quality file drawers are the perfect size for storing bulky clothing, blankets, pillows, and comforters in your office. However, don't use a metal file drawer to store anything that snags easily. In order to avoid disturbing guests, never store linens for other rooms in a space where you expect guests to sleep.
- When covering a radiator, extend the unit as far as possible on either side to create open or doored storage—and to carry the eye across a long, unified line.
- Placing a home office as close as possible to an outside door and in a room with—or next to—a bathroom helps maintain a professional aura. (It's also the nicest arrangement for overnight guests.)
- Collect baskets and interesting boxes to conceal and bring order to the gizmos every multipurpose room collects—nothing makes a TV room or library feel so inadequate as having to leave it to get your nail file or a cordless toothbrush.

Avoiding the Obvious

It's hard to think of this space as a "spare" room, since its owner needed it to carry out three critical functions: home office, guest room, and household storage. The usual storage solution, a massive wall of floor-to-ceiling units, was out of the question here; it would have unduly narrowed, indeed overwhelmed, an already narrow room.

ABOVE: Separate base cabinets and wall-hung cabinets, including a combination dresser/desk unit, leave a wide, long, free strip. Mirroring the wall between the upper and lower cabinets creates a feeling of depth, and installing lights above and below the top cabinets lets them "float," further counteracting any overwhelming impression this much cabinetry might convey. The lower lights double as task lighting at the desk.

The highly reflective, horizontally striped surface on the cabinets, repeated in the wall-end mirror, emphasizes the length of the wall. The horizontal lines of the accordion-pleated window shade create a balance by broaden-ing the far wall. The lights over the cabinets and the up-lift torchère on the right give a lift to the ceiling. Without the illusion of a lifted ceiling, the extensive use of horizontal lines would have been overbearing in this small a space.

The tailored, tucked-in cover on the double bed carries the boldest pattern in the room, but it takes up less space—both visually and physically—than a traditional flowing bedspread. Diagonal placement and a frame lifted on legs and upholstered in fabric that complements the carpet make the bed a second "floating" element in the room.

Family and Guests

The family that lives in this apartment wanted the most gracious extra bedroom possible for frequent overnight guests, but also needed overflow space for its library and art collection. Then, too, family members wanted a room where they could occasionally escape to read, reflect, or nap.

BELOW: The elegant form of a sleigh bed always makes it appropriate for double duty as a sofa or chaise longue. The cream and blue color scheme enlarges the space by recalling sunshine and blue sky. When not in use for reading, the slim brass lamps turn sideways to illuminate the outer extremes of the room. The ceiling border draws the eye upward from framed art of the same hues, and calls attention to the additional space above the tall bookcases, which were store bought and custom stained to match the rosewood bed.

The caned armchair is as inviting as an upholstered piece, but less bulky. The glass-top side table barely exists visually, yet provides a generous surface for snacks, books, and writing materials. The solid, plush wall-to-wall carpet picks up the rosy tones of the wood to increase the sense of spaciousness. The curtain is partially drawn to hide an ugly view and direct the eye to the better view out the other side of the window.

Smoothing-over Strange Shapes

The only space this family could spare for its library, home office, and family room was not only narrow but strangely shaped: a bulky, obtrusive structural column separated the windows in the room and created a large amount of what appeared to be unusable space.

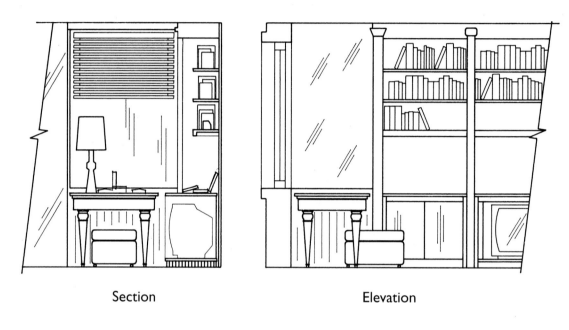

Section   Elevation

Desk and Bookcase Wall

FACING PAGE: The home office consists of a delicate antique desk, placed in a squared-off niche with a single window, and a typewriter shelf in a wall of bookcases set at a right angle to the desk. The bookcases are lifted on legs so the eye won't mistake them for the perimeter of the room.

The mirrored wall between the window and the bookcase reflects outdoor light and views, making the niche feel larger than it actually is and more psychologically comfortable to work in. The wheeled ottoman can swivel from desk to typewriter, and slips under the desk when not in use. The structural column is mirrored to augment the sense of spaciousness on the desk side and make the room in general appear as though it has an uninterrupted expanse of window.

Simple pleated shades in the same color as the wall allow in maximum daylight without drawing the eye to the strange configuration, as a bolder window treatment might. The fortuitous reflection of a door into an adjacent space adds a sense of depth.

A roll-out TV shelf in the base of one of the bookcases conserves space (low placement of the TV is said to be the most restful for eye and neck muscles (see page 56). Other furnishings also impart a sense of visual space: an armchair with spare, simple legs; an armless sofa that provides an extra foot or so of seating while cutting down on bulk. A second tier on the coffee table makes room for extra books, an attaché case, and a basket to hide some of the miscellaneous odds and ends that tend to collect in a triple-use room.

Wall-to-wall carpeting in a small pattern and a subtle color that blends with the upholstery helps create a roomy feeling. In a pinch, the back cushions can be removed from the sofa in order to make it up as a single bed for an overnight guest, giving this tiny space yet a fourth use.

Home and Office in One

A full-time consultant needed this room, not much more than 12 feet wide, as a professional office and meeting space for clients, *and* as a guest room *and* an exercise room *and* storage space for out-of-season clothes, sports equipment, empty luggage, mementos, old business and personal files, household tools, and office stationery.

ABOVE: Floor-to-ceiling mirrors visually double the size of the space and relieve the consultant of the sensation that she is constantly working up against the wall. Facing mirrors on the structural columns in the corners make the room look as though it has four large windows instead of just one. The furniture in the meeting area is deliberately low to avoid blocking the room-expanding views.

Built-in wall-length supply cabinets provide enough surface room for a full computer setup, but are stepped back to create more room in the seating area. The wall-hung cabinets hold a small library and a large array of electronic equipment. Strip lighting illuminates the work surface. The metal open frame of the desk chair permits it almost to disappear. A supplementary library is tucked under the window. A carpet pattern that resembles perforated metal lends a sense of airiness to the room.

As shown in the floor plan, a generous square cut out of the far end of the room serves as a walk-in closet, while an existing almost-unusable corner is the perfect fit for an attractive, compact stationary exercise machine.

There is no suggestion to clients that this strictly business space turns into a guest room when the lightweight occasional table is moved and the love seat opened to a double bed.

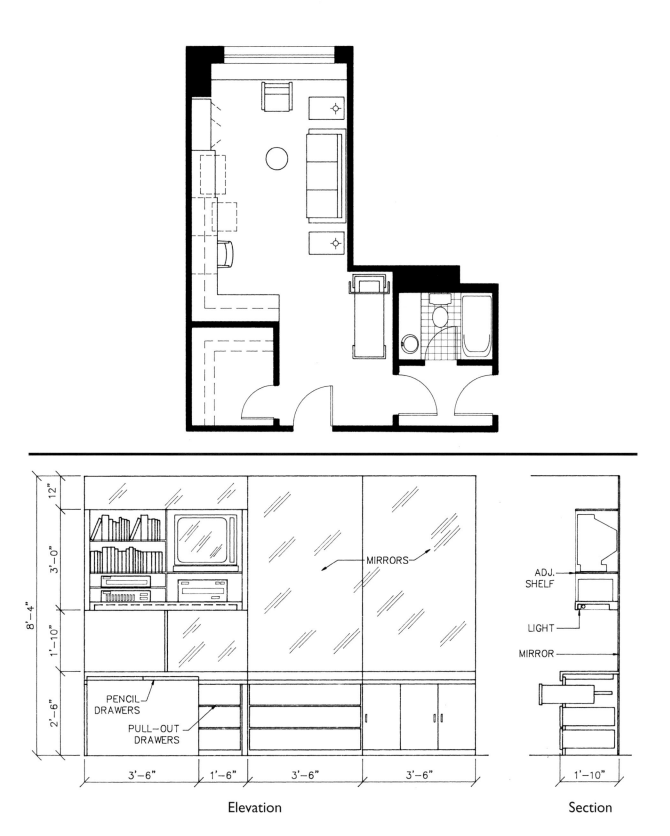

MIRRORS

PENCIL DRAWERS

PULL-OUT DRAWERS

12"

3'-0"

1'-10"

2'-6"

8'-4"

3'-6"   1'-6"   3'-6"   3'-6"

Elevation

ADJ. SHELF

LIGHT

MIRROR

1'-10"

Section

Den/Office Wall Unit

Color Me Bold

Bold, invigorating colors were the home owners' preference for this den/library, but the space was an incredibly tiny ten-foot square. Bold and dark colors usually reduce the visual space in a room. In this case, however, the color scheme could be offset by a number of space-making strategies.

LEFT: Sandwiched between the vibrant large-pattern carpet and the intense blue ceiling, with its deep green crown molding, are pale gray walls, which seem to float outward. The well-padded armchair has a large presence, but it has slender legs and the upholstery blends into the color of the wall.

The heavily green and red color scheme is an especially fresh complement to natural woods. Translucent shoji-screened double doors are a delicate, airy, and more inviting alternative to bulkier, opaque standard doors.

A thin strip of the wall unit's lighter color carried throughout the room beneath the green molding helps to unify all the visual contrasts. The gray mirrored backs of the bookshelves also help expand the sense of space.

Although the custom cabinetry covers an entire wall, the simplicity of its design—ten inches deep with exposed uprights, glass shelves, and moldings that conceal downlighting—makes it a better fit for the room than bulkier, store-bought units would have been.

PART TWO

Lighting

Architectural lighting design developed as an off-shoot of the theater, where light has always been used to help stages appear large enough to contain battlefields, ballrooms, town squares, and other places capable of holding a cast of thousands. On the stage, lighting also reminds actors where they are supposed to be and what they are supposed to be doing. At its most basic, it keeps them from tripping over the scenery or falling off the stage.

So, too, in the home, where lighting effects can seem to raise the ceiling, dissolve the walls, attract the gaze to distant reaches, and gloss over tight spots. A light in a curio cabinet can draw attention to its contents and at the same time emphasize that care should be taken in the immediate vicinity. During a party, slightly dimmer light in a home-office alcove can keep the space visually connected to the adjoining room but subtly discourage guests from gathering around the desk. Professional lighting designers say that glitter and sparkle make people wittier than they normally would be.

No matter how creative the lighting, it must also prevent accidents by keeping us aware, for instance, of the location of steps and objects that could be tripped over or knocked over. Likewise, any light-created illusion that could cause accidents—for example, the illusion of a step could just as easily cause people to trip as a poorly lit real step—must be avoided. For people with poor eyesight, lighting may also have to indicate something as simple as where the floor ends and the walls begin.

The overall glow that helps us identify obstacles within a room is generally called *ambient lighting*. Ambient lighting doesn't call attention to anything in particular. It just washes over the space, helping us to orient ourselves and forming a background for more practical or dramatic effects. It also seems to dematerialize bulk and lets surfaces and objects appear to merge into one another. All by itself, however, this homogenous glow can be somewhat dull.

Lighting for convenience is called *task lighting*. It is used in specific areas and covers specific tasks like reading, sewing, cooking, shaving and applying makeup, and watching TV. In a small bathroom, task lighting may also serve as ambient light, but most other task lights should be a somewhat stronger beam in an already glowing room. Task lights that glow all by themselves in the dark may create such extreme contrasts that eyestrain or accidents result.

Accent lighting, the stuff of illusion and the most important component of space making, comprises all the techniques that keep the eye moving around the space on long, smooth journeys. It picks out art works, architectural details, significant pieces of furniture, large stretches of space. It cues us as to what to look at and what route to take to the next object of interest. Ideally, it will skip over or distract attention away from anything that does not suggest spaciousness. It can appear to push walls away and make objects float. For both safety and illusion, it absolutely *must* be used in combination with ambient light.

Finally, *sparkle lighting* adds energy to a room. A little goes a long way—a couple of cut crystal sconces, the glint of light off sleek metal trim, pinpoints of light gleaming through a perforated surface. Whereas ambient light creates feelings of contentment, and accent light creates interest, sparkle light makes people happy to be in a room.

According to psychologists, 87 percent of what we learn and how we feel about what we learn comes through our eyes; therefore, the look of things can be more powerful than the things themselves. Applied to lighting design, this means, for instance, that naked bulbs, which give off an uncomfortable glare, should be hidden—behind a lamp shade or sconce, under the bottom lip of a cabinet, behind molding at the top of a bookcase or wall, inside a dropped ceiling or custom-built soffit, or in a floor mounting directed away from normal gaze. The only naked bulbs that should be in full view are those in chandeliers (which must be kept dimmed down to a sparkly accent and not depended on to identify food on the table), bulbs such as neon strips, or tiny sparklers that are considered art work. Don't go overboard, however, in concealing light sources; many people feel distinctly uneasy in rooms where *all* the light comes from mysterious sources. Lighting designers suggest that there be at least one visible fixture—a table or floor lamp, a pendant, a sconce—in every room, even if the majority of the light comes from hidden sources.

For the more dramatic illusions, the ones that actually change perceptions of space, consider:

- Light directs attention to objects, and makes the space (or the lack of space) around the objects lose importance. While it can't illuminate space per se, it can create the illusion of a lot of space between the objects it picks out.
- Light has almost no color of its own, and it tends to make the surfaces it touches paler and therefore seem even farther away. Anything it glows within will tend to float.

- Lighting can create ambiguity about the locations of physical boundaries. When ceiling and wall are in similar colors, for instance, light directed where they meet will almost erase the border and give the impression of a much higher ceiling.
- Lighting dark corners, alcoves, and niches can make them appear larger. On the other hand, leaving these areas dark can make it seem as though they have been deducted from the total perceived space in a room.
- A multipurpose family room will probably need more task lighting than any other room in your home. Wall and ceiling mounts are best in order to keep surfaces free. Small fixtures mounted in or on cabinetry make it easy to find stored materials and to use entertainment equipment.
- Lighting a window box or plants, or uplighting trees at the far end of a patio will expand space by seeming to pull the room out the window. Make sure you use special waterproof outdoor fixtures and connections.
- Lighting the insides of bookcases and open and glass-doored cabinets minimizes their overall mass and draws attention to their depth.
- In the bedroom, ceiling-mounted fixtures aimed at a pale closet door can do double duty—they can bounce soft light back into the room when the doors are closed and illuminate the contents of the closet when the doors are opened. Extended reading requires both soft task light and adequate background light. Little lamps that clip onto a book cause eye fatigue and make the room close in.
- Lights tucked under the front of upper kitchen cabinets can help make them seem to disappear, but an overhead light is still necessary to help find utensils and ingredients stored in the cabinets. To avoid glare, use an uplight pendant that bounces light off the ceiling or a ceiling mount with a diffuser lens.
- Tucking light fixtures under beds or built-in furniture lifts the pieces up and expands the sense of floor space.
- A chandelier or pendant over a dining table can stop the eye several feet short of the room's actual boundaries. To achieve the same—or better—lighting and at the same time expand the space, try wall sconces and ceiling-mounted fixtures. An

adjustable ceiling fixture also will make it possible for you to keep the light focused on the table even if you add leaves or push one end against a wall (see "Living and Dining Rooms").

- The sharp scallop effects—or arch shapes—that downlights can produce on walls may be attractive, but they tend to be the kind of attention grabbers that can keep the eye from registering the rest of the room. To avoid scallops, keep light sources three feet from the wall, use frosted diffusers, use wider beams and overlapped beams, or try the silver-tipped bulbs that cut out the hot spot in the middle of the beam.

- If your lighting is completely even, all the light in a room becomes equally unimportant. Instead, use moderate levels of brightness for general or ambient lighting, higher levels for tasks and accents, and low levels for glitter. In addition, keep the eye moving by installing light sources on three planes: up by the ceiling, at elbow-to-shoulder height, and near the floor (try uplight cans, strips of light under low cabinetry, even neon or fiber-optic strips in the joint between wall and floor).

- At the touch of a finger, dimmers and controls can change the mood of a room: the place by the kitchen where the kids congregate to do their homework suddenly becomes an intimate bistro; the place where you put your feet up to watch TV becomes an elegant salon; your home office becomes an upscale bar; the bathroom becomes a posh powder room or a relaxing spa. Dimming a light to "off" is also less jarring than simply using a switch.

- More light may be needed in a room filled with dark, light-absorbing colors—including the clothes of party-goers; as more dark-clad guests arrive, up the wattage a bit, or your fascinating gathering may turn into nothing but a milling crowd.

- If you think you are going to need professional lighting design services, it's best to arrange for this before making any decisions about any other design element. Structural changes—dropping a ceiling, for example, or breaking into a wall—may be suggested by a lighting designer. When lighting designers are hired after most of the other work is done, they usually find themselves creating illusions to cover up mistakes rather than helping to expand space. Just make sure the lighting designer understands that space making is a major concern. Clue him or her in on any visual problems household members may have, and be specific about how much heat you can tolerate from light bulbs.

IMAGINARY SPACE

ABOVE: A major focal point of this room—a line sculpture of blue neon—is actually not in the room at all but on the far wall of the entry foyer. One neon triangle hugs the wall and another the ceiling, forming a glowing pyramid that draws the eye upward. The angles of the form also help to expand the space by creating the illusion of a corner that seems to shift the end of the foyer back a foot or so.

Three long faux windows were cut into the wall behind the chairs, filled with translucent glass, and spot lit from behind, making it seem possible to step through the openings into the outdoors.

BELOW: Reflected in the mirrored wall, the open-cage lighting system over the banquette becomes a sculpture floating in space. Avoiding the cost of creating a new electrical junction box directly behind the fixture, black wire connects it with a black backplate over the existing box in a deliberate swag formation. The low-voltage adjustable fixtures can plug into the cage at almost any point.

Budget considerations also led to the use of a pipe extending along the ceiling from the kitchen ceiling fixture to provide electricity for the adjustable pendant over the dining table and for the spot light. The pipe was deliberately painted a bold black; painted the color of the ceiling, it would still show and look like a design compromise.

Fluorescent task lighting for the kitchen is tucked under the cabinets, while a ceiling fixture (not seen here) maintains a consistent lighting mood that psychologically joins the space of the kitchen to the living/dining room.

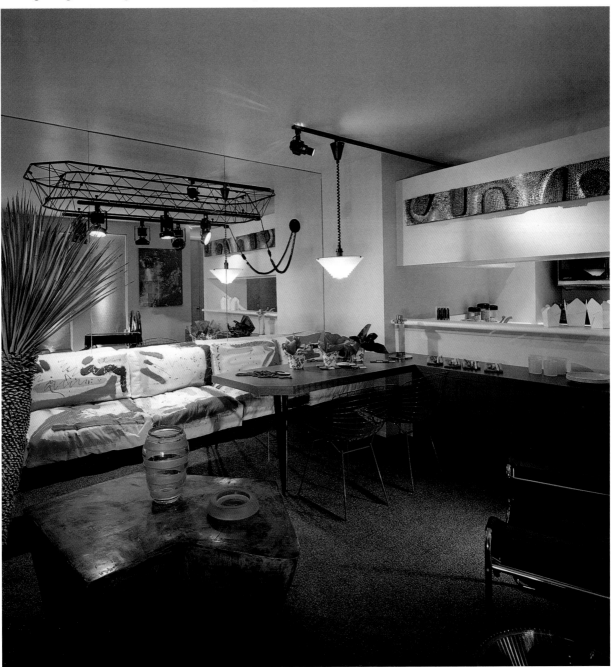

TYPES OF BULBS

Incandescents

A lamps are the traditional clear or frosted light bulbs that let light shine out in all directions, including places where you don't necessarily want or need light. They are best for table and floor lamps and for sconces. They are inexpensive to buy, and come in a wide variety of brightnesses. Most people are very fond of the light they provide—a tiny bit yellower than actual daylight—and associate it with the notion of "home."

Reflector bulbs have reflective silver coating on the part near the socket; light is captured and directed out through the uncoated part. Ellipsoidal reflectors, or ER bulbs, can deliver up to twice as much brightness as bare bulbs of the same wattage. They are ideal for recessed downlights and "cans" on tracks, fixtures that otherwise just trap light coming out of the back end of ordinary bulbs and let it burn up the components without using it for any good purpose. Reflectors come in a variety of shapes that control the width of the beam of light. *Narrow spots* are good for picking out objects and for washing out the boundaries between wall and ceiling or wall and floor, but focused on a wall they will create harsh "scallops." *Regular spots* also are good for blurring boundaries, and form softer scallops on walls; overlapping beams from regular spots can help erase scallops. *Floods* and *narrow floods* (a term even professionals laugh at) produce wider beams and the softest scallop effects.

Low-voltage halogens are tiny bulbs that allow for smaller fixtures, tighter direction control, and easy hiding. They provide more intensity than standard or reflector incandescents. Halogens require transformers, usually built into the fixture, to adjust their voltage. For track systems, it is possible to purchase a transformer for each fixture to be attached, to buy a track that includes a transformer, or to buy a separate transformer the size of a shoe box that can be hidden in a wall or a closet to keep the visible components as sleek as possible.

Halogens are expensive and, since they are purchased mainly to provide an intensely focused, brilliant, cool white light up to 500 watts, the most expensive to use. Since they are filled with halogen or xenon gas, their filaments last longer than those in ordinary incandescents. Usually seen in minimalist contemporary fixtures, halogens recently have begun to show up in more traditional fittings, too.

Low-voltage halogens include the little MR16s that come encased in their own miniature reflector housings and produce beams that vary in width from extremely narrow to very, very wide. Despite the intense heat halogens produce, MR16s are favored for lighting art—most of the heat comes out the back of the lamp and is directed away from the object being lit. (See "Fiber Optics," below, for other art options. If you want special "picture lights," make sure they are labeled specifically for art.) Never, ever buy an MR16 that doesn't have a built-in lens on the front to protect you from hot flying glass in the event that overheating causes the tiny bulb to explode.

All incandescents burn out relatively quickly and use high levels of energy, which makes them the most expensive to operate. They also create great heat, which can be uncomfortable and drive up your air-conditioning bill.

PAR lamps have built-in reflectors, are larger than halogens, and tend to cast a warmer light. Some use low voltage, some use regular voltage. They produce less glare and provide somewhat more brightness per watt than ordinary light bulbs. They are ideal for downlighting fixtures.

High-intensity discharge bulbs, which include mercury vapor, metal halide, and high-pressure sodium, have been used traditionally in industrial situations or such nonresidential locations as parking lots. They can cut energy costs more significantly than any other type of light source. Recent developments in size and color control have brought some of these bulbs indoors into commercial and retail establishments, but the intensity of the light is still too great for residential use.

Fluorescents

Fluorescents use one third the energy of incandescents, last far longer, and give off the least heat when lit, but are not available in great brightnesses. They require ballasts, built into either the fixture or the bulb, to provide the high initial voltage to start the bulb and regulate the current. Magnetic or electromagnetic ballasts create a flicker on start-up and may hum or buzz. Electronic ballasts provide a quick, quiet, flicker-free start-up, and require less electricity; some may have built-in dimming for tubes (currently, dimmers can destroy compact fluorescents).

In the past, fluorescents had a way of making everything and everyone in their path look worn out and dreary, but recent developments in the mixture of color phosphors that coat the inside of the glass have resulted in more choices: warmer light, light that approximates daylight, and clear, cool light. The results are measured in kelvins (K) and are usually listed on the packaging; the range is from 2,700 K at the warm end, to 3,500 K in the neutral zone, to 4,100 K in the cool zone, and to 5,000 K at the very cool end. Check labels also for color-rendering index, or CRI: the higher the number (100 is the highest), the more natural the color of objects will appear; the lower the CRI, the greater the risk that colors will appear "off." To give an idea of why color matters—the incandescents we all love are 2,700 K to 3,000 K and have a CRI of 95; currently, fluorescents can go as high 5,000 K and as high 82 CRI (some older stock may be as low as 52 CRI). Color rendering may also be expressed in the letters RE (rare earth phosphors), followed by numbers; look for the highest first digit you can find—for example, RE8 gives objects a truer color than RE7 does.

Fluorescent tubes provide the widest variety in the tone of light, from extremely cool white to daylight to yellow. From time to time an import will appear on the market that makes objects of one color or another particularly intense. Fluorescent tubes come in two-, three-, four-, five-, and eight-foot lengths, and are ideal for indirect lighting—to create space near the ceiling or under shelving, for instance—or as task lighting over the counter in the kitchen. The ballast is included in the fixture, which may also include a reflector.

For indirect lighting installed above eye level, hide a fluorescent tube behind a strip of wood, drywall, or molding at least one inch deeper than the fixture itself; with fluorescent tubes now reduced to as little as $^1/_2$-inch in diameter, you won't lose much physical space, but you will gain a tremendous amount of psychological space.

Compact fluorescents are available in several colors. Some are available with screw-in bases to fit table and floor lamps. They are not available in such intense brightnesses as incandescents and are much more expensive, but local utilities sometimes offer incentives for their use. The ballast is usually included in the bulb, which is what makes it so heavy; some have separate ballasts that screw into the lamp and accept a plug-in bulb. A few compact fluorescents come with diffusers, lenses, and built-in or separate reflectors (the built-ins do a better job). Since they last for years, they are an ideal replacement for incandescents in hard-to-reach track, and ceiling-mounted or recessed fixtures—just make sure the fixtures are well ventilated so that heat buildup doesn't interfere with the compact fluorescent's performance. At present, there is no way to dim them without the risk of destroying them.

Neons

Neons don't emit the kind of light needed for general lighting purposes, but their intense colors and the fact that their tubes can be bent into almost any shape make them ideal for directing attention—or for distraction. Transformers and switches can be hidden.

Fiber Optics

Fiber-optic systems carry light from a strong hidden source through tiny strands of glass or plastic to provide a glow, but no heat or ultraviolet rays, elsewhere in the room. They provide good color and are ideal for protecting art from fading or deterioration. The bright ends of fiber-optic strands can be left free for overall glitter effects, or can be gathered into tiny fixtures that are ideal for focusing on art. Since fiber-optic strands glow all along their surfaces, they can also be used to create a neon effect. The source, smaller than a shoe box, can be hidden in a nearby closet or cabinet drawer.

DISAPPEARING BOUNDARIES

ABOVE: Two simple types of lighting fixtures combine to expand the physical boundaries of the dining section of this tiny room. A concave section of a dropped soffit holds two pairs of recessed downlights that shed gently scalloped pools of light on the back wall. Although scallops usually have the effect of shrinking a room, here they are softened by a small 500-watt uplight, which casts a complementary upward scallop and, in the process, dissolves the ceiling line. This kind of uplight fixture—which permits light to escape to the sides as well as upward—was chosen to create a broadening band of light across the wall above eye level. A chandelier or pendant lamp over the table would have stopped the eye before it could register the illusion of a deeper and higher space than the rest of the room. All the dining area fixtures are on dimmers that can be adjusted to balance the degree of daylight that streams through the living room window.

SECRET SOURCES

FACING PAGE: The two table lamps at the ends of the radiator cover function like the proverbial candles in the window, but they are not the only source of sunny glow in this living/dining room. The radiator cover itself incorporates a series of fluorescent tubes that light up the lower wall while at the same time dissolving it as a boundary. Fluorescent tubes tucked above and below the wall-hung bookshelf over the dining table seem to push the wall back; the upper tubes seem to raise the ceiling plane. A floor or table lamp in this area would have called attention to itself and therefore to the closeness of sofa and dining table.

In lieu of a chandelier or pendant, which would have grabbed too much attention, an unobtrusive adjustable spot was installed on the ceiling above the table; the reflector controls and directs the beam.

INVENTING A PATIO DOOR

ABOVE: A full-length closet, which made it difficult to envision the end of this space as a living room, was turned into an illusionary patio door through the use of backlighting behind shoji-style doors. Daylight fluorescent tubes—covered with plastic diffusers to protect clothes from even the minimal heat generated by the fluorescents—run along the closet ceiling and floor close to the doors. The diffusers also protect the lower tube from damage if anything should fall down from the closet shelves.

A mirrored covering helps erase the structural column at the end of the closet and extends the patio-door-like effect. The glow on the other side of the column comes from a frosted glass wall sconce (not visible here) mounted in a shallow recess.

Preprogrammed computer-controlled dimmers mimic the natural fluctuations of light during the day when household members are at home, turn everything off during the hours when they are away, and turn evening-level light on just before the first person is scheduled to arrive home.

FIXTURES

Recessed Downlights

Depending on the fixture size, recessed downlights require between 4^1/$_2$ inches and 14 inches of space above the ceiling line or in custom-built dropped soffits. They can be directed straight down, at a wall, or toward an object or grouping of objects ranging from figurines to furniture. Either the fixture or the bulb should have a glass lens to control the color and texture of the light and prevent uncomfortable glare.

Track Lighting

Unlike recessed downlights, track lighting does not require expensive digging above the ceiling plane or custom soffits, and permits the use of visibly decorative fixtures, including pendants. Since fixtures simply plug into the track, it is possible to have a wide variety in operation at one time and to do fast switches for special occasions. You can even combine ambient, accent, task, and glitter fixtures all on the same track.

(continued from bottom of page 110)

Track and fixtures—everything but the bulb—can be painted to match or contrast with the surroundings.

Surface Mounts

Surface-mounted lighting is permanently attached to one spot on the wall or ceiling, but can be adjusted to help direct light to a number of different locations. If you don't have an electrical junction box exactly where you want to create light, there are options: you can cut into the ceiling or wall to install one; you can fashion a new ceiling or wall section to hide the box; you can run a wire from the nearest outlet and conceal it with a plastic or metal wire cover; or you can install an adjustable fixture at the nearest existing junction box and swivel it to direct light where you need it.

Freestanding Lamps and Shades

Table lamps should have the bulb dead center in the middle of the shade to avoid glare when people are sitting under it or standing near it. For the same reason, the bottom of the shade should never be above the eye level of a seated person. Shades can be made up in the fabric or paper of your choice—just look up lamp shades in the telephone book to find a fabricator. If you love a shade that seems to be available only if you purchase the base, too, show a picture of it to a few fabricators. As a last resort, ask the manufacturer if you can buy the shade separately. If the lamp is part of the ambient lighting scheme, use a translucent shade; for tasks, an opaque shade with a white interior will do a better job of capturing and directing light.

In many cases, the type of bulb and the wattage is determined by the type of fixture, its materials, and design. If you prefer a certain type of bulb for aesthetic or budget reasons, make this clear to sales people as you do your shopping for fixtures.

THE CHANGING EYE

As we age, we require more light, but at the same time we find glare increasingly disorienting. The iris and cornea admit less light, and the lens begins to add a yellowish tinge to what we see and to interfere with perceptions of contrast by scattering light to the wrong parts of the retina. The aging processes begin at birth, and it's next to impossible to have a long life without some inconvenient eye problems. By age sixty, it's perfectly normal for the retina to receive as little as one third the light it did at age twenty.

To compensate, try:

- Substantially increased task lighting.
- A small increase in ambient lighting.
- Special care to keep unshielded light from leaking from fixtures directly outward to the eye—for instance, from the bottom or top of a table-lamp shade, or from gaps in a sconce cover.
- Opaque shades with white interiors for table or floor lamps that double as task lighting.
- Matte finishes on surfaces, to cut reflected glare.
- Different tones on different surfaces so that it's easy to distinguish where one surface ends and another begins—especially important on steps.
- Avoidance of shadows that simulate nonexistent objects—climbing a step that isn't there can produce just as bad a fall as missing one that is.
- Well-lit paths from bed to bath, with switches that can be activated on both ends of the journey.
- Switchless fixtures that respond when you touch them. Some can produce three or four light levels.
- Maximum dimming of chandeliers.
- Triphosphor fluorescents to bolster color in closets, kitchens, baths, and wherever medications are taken.
- Gray and blue (rather than bronze or even peach) window glass and mirrored wall tints.
- Awnings and electronically controlled window treatments to temporarily block outdoor glare, which is worst in the winter months, when the sun is low on the horizon.

THE FLOATING BED

BELOW: The most striking feature in this bedroom is a full-size bed that sems to float in air. Crown molding hides blue neon strips tucked under the platform; mirrors covering the base of the bed reflect and magnify the light. The effect is even more open than using a raised, legged bed would be. The neons are on dimmers so that they can function as night-lights during sleeping hours.

The floor-level lighting begins a long, strong upward diagonal that ends in the ceiling glow that comes from the table lamp on the radiator cover. The top shelf of the bookcase is lit with a small fluorescent tube behind the crown molding; it and an identical bookcase treatment on the opposite side of the window (not seen in this view) combine with the glow on the ceiling to create an arc of light high up at the far end of the room.

LACQUERED WOOD
MOLDING FRAME

6"
8 1/2"
6"

Section of Bed Base

FLUORESCENT LAMP

MIRROR

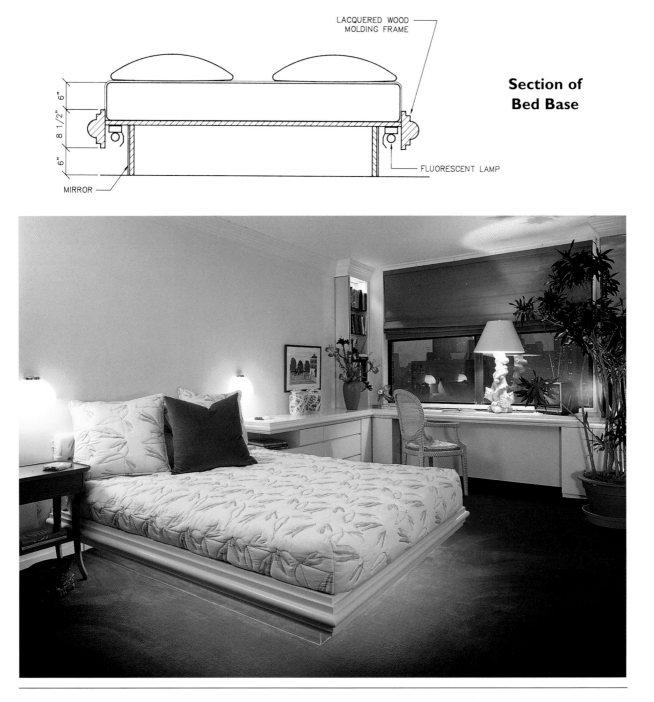

ENHANCING THE VIEW

ABOVE: This dining room was created out of a tiny bedroom. A French door was installed to visually connect the room with the rest of the home, and the closet was turned into a serving center.

The crown molding at the edge of the service center shelf hides two light sources—a blue neon strip the same color as in the nighttime sky to showcase glass and silver pieces, and a cool white fluorescent for daytime or when a natural glow is needed for the display of food. These lights, and the gray mirrors lining the back wall of the service center, expand the room by reflecting the dramatic view out the window. Ceramic uplight sconces keep illumination high in the corners.

The table is lit from above by a spotlight that can be adjusted quickly if the table is moved—to the side for buffet service, for instance.

LIGHTING FOR TELEVISIONS

Ambient and indirect lighting are best for TV viewing. A totally dark room may make the picture look quite brilliant, but it can cause eyestrain (and temporary blindness when you leave the room). Avoid reflected light from table lamps or directional downlights; it can be annoying and ultimately fatiguing to the eyes.

ELONGATING THE FLOOR

FACING PAGE: The light flooding out from under this built-in banquette emphasizes the flow of floor right up to the back wall. A simple two-inch piece of wood running the length of the underside of the banquette directs the light down rather than out and shields the fluorescent tube from view. Black closed-end fixtures mounted on the upper molding direct beams of light from compact fluorescents to the art on the walls. The pillar is covered with black glass, which minimizes its bulk while emphasizing its architectural qualities. The devices for attaching the banquette were in place before the glass was installed.

On the other side of the room, a ceiling track with movable, adjustable fixtures runs directly above the eating counter. The long track visually divides the dining and seating areas of the room without blocking views or taking up any space.

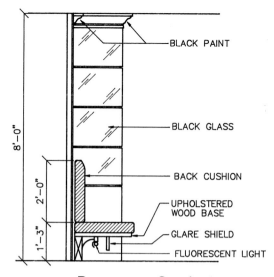

BLACK PAINT

BLACK GLASS

BACK CUSHION

UPHOLSTERED WOOD BASE

GLARE SHIELD

FLUORESCENT LIGHT

8'-0" 2'-0" 1'-3"

Banquette Section

DIMMERS AND CONTROLS

Dimmers and controls work together and often come packaged in the same system, but they have different functions.

Dimmers simply make the light from specific bulbs brighter or softer. Dimmers can be used with fluorescent tubes, but the light provided will be less than the tube's full brightness and there may be flickering. Compact fluorescents have not been usable on dimmers up to now, but as they are becoming more popular greater efforts are being made to develop the appropriate technology.

The wattage capacity listed on a dimmer represents the combined total of all the fixtures wired to the same dimmer; if the total wattage exceeds that specified on the dimmer, it will burn out. For residential use, the maximum wattage is 700.

Controls turn lights on and off singly, by group, by room, or throughout the entire house. They can be computer coded to go on and off at specified times,

they can be programmed to turn on at dusk and turn off at dawn, and they can be preset to respond to different situations—for example, you can flick one switch for a party setting, rather than going from room to room adjusting each individual fixture. Controls also can be useful when you don't want to fully light each room but, perhaps, want to illuminate a path from the front door to the kitchen to the bathroom, making access quicker after a long day at work. A main control by your bed can be used to light up the entire house if you hear a strange noise at night. Controls may be combined with burglar and smoke alarms to scare away intruders or enable quick escapes.

Don't keep the dimmers and controls for a room all on one switch; put ambient sources on one switch, accent lighting on another, and pathways on a third.

The best locations for switches are at entrances and by the bed or the sofa.

SWITCHING PLACES

ABOVE: Most people feel obliged to locate their dining areas wherever ceiling wiring already exists for a hanging lamp—after all, opening the ceiling to search for a new electrical connection is both costly and messy. In this living/dining room, however, the seating and dining areas were able to switch places through the use of a simple ceiling track that carries power directly from a junction box in an adjacent closet to the new dining area.

A simple, adjustable-focus downlight can was chosen to be used on the track; a chandelier or pendant would have shortened the room and obstructed the space-enhancing mirrored wall sections as well. The built-in dining room seating consists of foam cushions atop a carpeted plywood shelf fitted with a lip that hides fluorescent tubes. When the table is pushed to one side and the lamp refocused, the seating can be incorporated back into the living area. Plugged into an outlet on the same side of the room as the power source for the ceiling track, the under-shelf fluorescents carry a long line of light across the far end of the room, visually lifting the seating weight off the floor.

BREAKING THE RULES

BELOW: This narrow living/dining room is a good example of the benefits of breaking design rules—in this case, the rule against severely scalloped lighting. Here, the downlights are deliberately allowed to cast a hard-edged arch effect that seems to dissolve the wall as a boundary and sets up the impression of an arcade somewhere behind the actual wall line.

The built-in soffit containing the downlights circles out over the dining area to formally separate it from the seating area without using bulky dividers. The recessed lights are on preprogrammed dimmers that, with one push of a button, can soften the lighting during formal meals or provide just enough light for a safe entrance at night by targeting only the art. Since the use of floor lamps would have broken up the flow of space, reading light comes from wall sconces (not visible here) installed behind the sofa.

LIGHTING FOR COMPUTERS

Since computer screens reflect light, they can make the operator tired, headachy, and tense. Task lighting should be located below eye level, to the side of paperwork, and far enough back so that it isn't reflected on the screen. The light level should be as close to the intensity of the screen as possible but not so dim that you can't comfortably read paper materials. The best solution may be to bounce the light away from you and off a pale back wall. Ambient lighting should be uniform, not too much darker than task light, and from a source that will not be reflected on the computer screen—depending on the computer's range of movement and the direction of your fixtures, you may not want to operate a computer in the vicinity of downlighting.

The best placement of the screen is perpendicular to the window; second best is with the operator facing the window and the screen facing away from it. Some computer screens are impossible to read in bright sunlight, no matter what direction they face. Reflective surfaces near the computer can cause as much trouble as reflections on the screen; keep the work surface matte instead of glossy, and dark or medium toned instead of white.

UP AND AWAY

ABOVE: It's hard to believe this room resembled an alley before a number of design techniques—all of them ultimately dependent on lighting—were applied. The soft red neon "light art" near the ceiling, for instance, not only draws the eye upward but also reinforces the soffit that angles away from the window to frame a wall unit. The wall unit diminishes from 22 inches deep at the window end, to accommodate the full depth of the TV, to 12 inches at the near end, where it meets the mirrored wall that enlarges the dining area. The neon also helps to minimize the bulk of the unit, by directing attention to the wall behind it. A softened red was chosen to avoid grabbing attention away from the row of galvanized metal outdoor fixtures mounted high on the opposite wall. These fixtures were chosen for their sculptural effect as well as for their ability to cast an interesting pattern on the ceiling and highlight the art. The height of the fixtures draws attention up and away from the bulk of the sofa.

Floors

More than any other element in a room, the floor has to convince us that it is large and flowing. After all, if a floor seems small, why should we believe the room is big?

In general, floor coverings in pale neutral tones and small overall patterns will tend to make a room seem larger. But, design rules are made to be broken, so if you are bored by small neutral patterns, don't use them. There are many fool-the-eye techniques that can be used to create the illusion of more floor space, even with vivid colors and large patterns.

Our eyes naturally seek out the floor in any room we enter, if only because gravity makes it easy for our eye muscles to do so. Designers do everything they can to entice the eye upward and outward, to keep it moving from delight to delight, but the floor has to do its part, too, in order to keep up the illusion of wide open spaces. Remember: the longer it takes the eye to journey through a space, the larger the space registers in the mind; if a floor doesn't inspire the eye to keep roving around the entire space, it is probably not doing its job.

One way a floor can expand space is by using boldly contrasting colors or textures to create lines that lead the eye away from dead center. The same contrasts can also separate functional areas within a room without the use of bulky dividers. Flooring can

be laid at an angle to create longer lines for the eye to follow. Overall, floor coverings can be in whatever color and texture make us happiest, and still make a major contribution to the project of space creation. So, before opting for the recessive, small, neutral pattern, think about some of these possibilities:

- In a long, narrow room, use a strong directional pattern (for example, a striped carpet) parallel to the short wall to keep the eye from registering length as the dominant factor.
- Another technique to broaden a narrow room involves using the same color—or the same degree of lightness or darkness—in the flooring and in focal points on the opposing walls. This leads the eye from focal point to floor to second focal point and distracts from the shortest distance, that between the two walls. The most space-making effects occur when the surfaces between the floor and the focal points—wall space, furnishings—are in recessive cool or pale tones.
- Weatherproof floors like ceramic tile and granite can extend rooms outward onto balconies and patios. For protection against slipping, unglazed, unpolished surfaces are best.
- Patches of floor that don't contain furniture always give the impression of space to spare, and look larger when they feature a directional line—wood

planks, striped carpets, tiles laid in a diamond pattern.

- When baseboards, upholstery, lower walls, and furniture frames are in the same tones as the floor, the sense of floor space can be expanded anywhere from a few inches to a few feet into the vertical plane.

- Using a border of a different material—ceramic tile around carpet, for instance—can make the floor appear to be floating in a larger space.

SAFETY FIRST

Other chapters in this book encourage you to experiment as much as possible with nontraditional—even outrageous—materials and techniques, but flooring may be one area where it's best to stick with the tried and the true.

Why?

- A floor has to be safe for the people who walk on it. Unless you are positive that a nontraditional floor covering won't cause people to trip, stumble, slide, stub their toes, catch their heels, or cut their feet, don't even consider it.

- Undoing a failed flooring experiment is harder than correcting any other design component. You can easily repaint the walls or throw out the curtains, but to change a floor you generally have to move all the furniture—some of it quite heavy, some of it built in—out of the room and keep it out until a proper floor is installed.

- Current flooring options come in such a wide variety that the look you are trying to achieve may already exist in manufactured form. If not, it is usually perfectly safe to experiment with combining different flooring products—their safety, durability, and installation methods are already well known, so you can't go too far wrong. Any kind of flooring can be used as an insert into any other kind of flooring. As long as care is taken to ensure that both materials are at the same level to avoid tripping, sections of stone can be inserted into carpeting, carpeting can be inserted into vinyl, wood can be inserted into ceramic tile, and so on. The extra care that is needed in polishing areas where one material meets another can be worth it, especially where a combination is used to differentiate one functional area from another. Whenever carpet and a hard flooring surface butt up against each other, shoes, furniture, and cleaning equipment tend to bang up against the harder material; to prevent chipping, make sure a thin metal strip is installed around the edges.

TYPES OF FLOORING

Vinyl Flooring

Vinyl floors permit the easiest care, greatest durability, and most variety—including mixing and inlaying—of any of the synthetic floors. Vinyl is also easier on the feet than wood or stone and probably causes less fatigue than any other kind of flooring.

Vinyl sheet goods come in 4- to 12-foot widths; for a seamless look, the joints can be hidden under appliances or built-ins, or in the dark edges of the flooring's pattern. Vinyl in sheet form is softer on the feet than vinyl tile. Vinyl sheet goods provide large waterproof surfaces, but if water gets in around the edges, it could stagnate. The sheet form can easily be cut with a mat knife to butt up against the edges of free-form carpets. Look for no-polish products and investigate guarantees; before buying, check the edges to make sure that normal traffic won't wear off the color or pattern.

Vinyl tiles come in 12-inch squares, but can also be custom ordered in 6-inch, 9-inch, and 18-inch squares.

The best tiles have a layer of color and pattern on the bottom and a top layer of clear "self-healing" material that adds a bit of visual depth to the product. The second-best choice is a tile that carries color and pattern all the way through its thickness; no matter how much you walk off, there's still more

SQUARED-OFF HERRINGBONE

ABOVE: Laid on the diagonal so that the plank edges are parallel with the walls, this herringbone-patterned wood floor provides row upon row of "arrows" leading from the door to the farthest corner of the room. The floor's strongly colored wood stain was chosen to balance the mass of the sofa and the intensity of its upholstery. Although at first glance the sofa seems strikingly different from the rest of the room in color, pattern, and style, its orange hue actually mimics the floor's wood tone and fol-

lows the direction of one section of the herringbone. The strong wood stain also lets the freestanding pieces of traditional furniture blend into the floor, and encourages the contrasting pale walls to recede outward. The small area rug lends warmth to the hard floor, and, by its size, emphasizes the expanse of wood around it; it also anchors the furniture arrangement without making it difficult to shift pieces around. The custom desk beneath the window continues the wood tones up the wall; a pale-colored radiator cover exposed underneath it makes the desk look airy.

below it. The third option, a tile that has color and pattern only in a top layer, where it can wear or chip off in time, may still be suitable for areas that you plan to re-cover frequently.

Because tiles are slightly more brittle than sheet goods, they are not quite as easy underfoot, but it is possible to do some cutting in order to lay them in highly original patterns. Self-adhesive tiles are the easiest to lay, but they may begin to curl up in time; the adhesive backing also may lose power if the tile has been in the store too long.

Stone Flooring

Onyx, limestone, slate, marble, quartzite, and granite are all naturally quarried stones, but they differ in their hardness, durability, and ability to take and keep a high polish. They also differ in their vulnerability to stains, which are not easy to remove; a penetrating sealer can help prevent staining. Maintenance requires only a mop and a vacuum. If the finish becomes dull, granites and marbles can be repolished professionally. The

FACING PAGE: Bleached wood parquet flooring made it possible to turn this narrow living/dining room into a flowing space of the palest possible—but entirely natural—tones. The glossy polyurethane finish brings light into the middle of the space and makes it easy to keep the pale floor clean, especially in the dining area.

The matte ivory sectional that curves around a structural column into a bookcase/radiator cover, the pale, neutral wall pattern, the matte ceiling, and the curve of the sculpture all contribute to the flow of the room. All the freestanding furniture is open-framed to allow the floor's light to flow through, and curved to keep the eye moving smoothly. The recessed mirrored wall in the dining area creates the impression of a dining ell where there is none.

---

higher the polish, however, the slipperier the floor will be underfoot.

Stones come in tiles up to $^3/_4$ inch thick; stone thinner than $^3/_8$ inch is usually too fragile for a floor. Square stone tiles come in a variety of sizes and can be laser cut into irregular shapes to create inserts or overall original patterns. Stone is probably the most expensive type of flooring and has to be considered permanent in most cases; because the adhesive that holds stone tiles to the floor is a cement, these tiles tend to be destroyed in the process of removal. It may be possible to install them on small sections of Masonite subfloor that can be picked up and taken with you if you move, but there is no guarantee that some of the pieces won't crack anyway.

Because it is so hard, stone may not be the best choice for people who are accident prone or in households with very young children or any other unsteady people. At the least, the stone should probably be covered with carpet.

Onyx is the hardest—and most expensive—stone. Unlike the polished black onyx used in jewelry, onyx for flooring is off-white, green, or gold, with a translucent watery pattern. Bringing it to a high polish takes more labor than polishing granite or marble, but the effort is worth it because the finish will last longer and the onyx's color and pattern will be showcased.

Granite is not quite so hard or expensive as onyx, but like onyx it requires a high polish to reveal its color and pattern. Since granite can now be dyed, it is beginning to be seen in unusual and often brilliant tones.

Marble is moderately priced stone. Like those of onyx and granite, marble's color and pattern emerge when highly polished, but the finish wears off more quickly. It is more vulnerable to stains (which is why real marble is seldom seen in a kitchen counter), but cannot be dyed.

Slate, *quartzite*, and *limestone*, the least expensive types of stone, do not take a high polish and therefore have a natural slip resistance. Slate has a textured pattern and comes in a variety of shades—red, green, and gray, for instance. Quartzite comes in a variety of golds, beiges, and off-whites, sometimes with metal flecks. Limestone is available in different textures and designs and a variety of beige tones. All need a penetrating sealer to protect their surface and color.

Terrazzo is a composite material made of chips of a hard material—such as marble, glass, metal, or mother-of-pearl—embedded in a concrete or epoxy base. An entire seamless terrazzo floor can be poured on site at great expense, but the material also comes in a tile form that costs less than granite or marble. It can be highly polished or slightly textured and treated with a sealer. Unlike granite or marble, it can be filled and repolished if it happens to chip, but it does not hold a polish as well. Paradoxically, even though terrazzo is a man-made composite that can be designed to suit almost any decor, its random patterning can make it appear more natural than marble.

Ceramic Tile

Ceramic tiles are clay products that can be purchased in a wide variety of price categories depending on style and quality—you can even buy antique tiles. Installation costs, however, tend to be less costly than for stone, since tile can be cut to fit just like glass, by scoring it and snapping off the unneeded portion. Ceramic tile can be used for almost any effect—southwestern adobe, Byzantine mosaic, Dutch renaissance, Art Nouveau, sleek modern. Some tiles are available with skid-resistant finishes, and sizes range from 2-inch to 24-inch squares.

For really intricate floor designs utilizing smaller tiles, it is possible to draw a pattern on paper and send it to a computerized tile house that will redraw the design to fit your specifications and give you back precisely arranged tiles on large pieces of mesh backing. These larger components are much easier to install than a lot of small pieces. It may be best to do this through a professional designer or a large tile supply shop in order to get your measurements absolutely correct.

On the more economical side, it is possible to buy plain tile squares and use colored grout to carry out design concepts. Using a gap of no more than $1/4$ inch between tiles, you can create an overall grid effect with a single color or a plaid effect with several colors; inscribe strong vertical or horizontal lines; gather groups of tiles within borders of complementary or contrasting grout; or just outline a few tiles in a random pattern.

Glazed tiles do not stain, but the grout does, even grout colored to match the tile. Treating grout with sealer every few years will help protect the color and keep dirt from infiltrating grout pores. A color wash can restore the original hue of unsealed grout or change white to another shade. Discolored pale grout can be bleached without damaging the tile, or it can be chipped out and replaced; removing it will not dislodge the tiles.

Mosaic

Mosaics are patterns, even pictures, fashioned from tiny pieces of marble, ceramic tile, and/or glass. The cost depends on the material—marble mosaic can run to $250 a square foot—and on whether you buy ready-made designs attached to mesh backing or design your own pattern with the help of a computer house. Small sections of mosaic flooring can be

MAXIMIZING OPEN SPACE

FACING PAGE: Wood plank installed on a diagonal creates longer lines for the eye to follow and lets the unoccupied portions of the floor appear larger than they are. The bleached tone and low-gloss finish of the flooring help the floor recede from the eight-foot ceiling, opening up plenty of visual space for bold alternations of orange pleated shades and mirrored columns.

The bronze-tinted mirrors raise the ceiling farther by carrying the taupe tones of the floor in a vertical line up the wall (a peach tint, on the other hand, would have created a horizontal continuation of wall covering and window treatment). The sofa upholstery mimics the tone and grain of the floor so that the impression of a wood border continues all the way around the rug. The shelved radiator cover is raised slightly off the floor to enhance the sense of floor space; the graduated shelf arrangement—12 inches deep at top, 15 inches in the center, 18 inches at the bottom—suggests a broad staircase leading up the wall.

CANCELING THE SHORTEST DISTANCE

ABOVE: In this long, narrow space, the large Oriental rug does more than just visually separate the living room from the wood-floored dining area; its rich, warm color creates a floor-level weight that prevents the eye from traveling on a straight line between the framed art on the side walls. Instead, the gaze moves in a curve from one picture downward to the floor and then up to the other picture. Even as the rug gathers the furniture into an intimate relationship, the pale, cool upholstery recedes to draw the eye away from the center. A smaller rug would only call attention to itself and the smallness of the space.

Placing the rounded end of the sectional on the wood floor—and installing a bold soffit above it—helps to create a triple-illusionary space that reads as a foyer, and extensions of both living room and dining room. The glass-top slim-framed coffee table has little perceived bulk and permits the rug pattern to shine through. (Note the delicate stone credenza, with its suggestion of a fireplace.)

installed on Masonite for easy portability if you move; if some of the tiny pieces pop off during removal, they can be put back in fairly easily.

Wood Flooring

Flooring automatically means wood to many of us. Until fairly recently, wood beams were part of the structural system of buildings, and wood was the easiest floor to attach to them.

Oak is hard, with a rough open grain. It takes stain and bleach well, but overfinishing can rob it of its distinctive grain.

Mahogany is a hardwood with a tight grain that makes it an appropriate choice for a sleek, smooth look. It has a good natural reddish-brown color and lends itself to a variety of darker stains.

Teak is a hardwood with a natural brown color

and a tight swirling grain that is best revealed by a low-gloss finish.

Wood comes in strips, blocks, or preassembled parquet squares that either butt up against each other or interlock; interlocking pieces create a stronger floor. When you buy, carefully check installation requirements: most of today's wood flooring, even long planks, can be installed directly on top of existing flooring.

Composition

Solid wood floors can be resanded and refinished for years, even generations, but they react to moisture; they expand slightly with high humidity, contract with prolonged dryness and central heating, and tend to curl and buckle when laid on or below grade—that is, on or below ground level,

NO DISTRACTIONS

FACING PAGE: Because this high-end commercial-grade carpet features a dense low pile that doesn't show footprints or vacuum marks, nothing distracts from the serene expanse of pale peach in this room—from the floor to the upholstery to the walls. The bold, spicy shade of the window treatment counteracts the strength of the view, which could make the otherwise pale room feel chilly.

PLAYING THE ANGLES

BELOW: Low-cut pile in a striped pattern can be laid diagonally, with the seams hidden along stripes in low-traffic areas. Placing the diagonal on the longest line in the room draws the eye the farthest distance, and also makes any empty floor spaces appear larger. Here, leggy furniture, a glass-top table, and a clear acrylic bar rack keep the line of vision stretching between the most massive pieces, the dining banquette and the sectional sofa. A directionless carpet—solid or with an overall pattern—would not have had the same spatial effect. Running the diagonal in the opposite direction—toward the smallest section of the room, the office tucked behind the dining set—wouldn't have worked either. Halfway to the ceiling, the diagonal is repeated in the cut-off of the custom light fixture over the table.

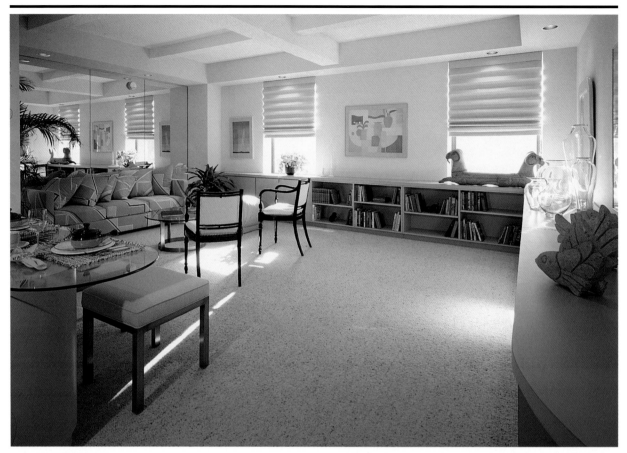

ROOM TO SPARE

ABOVE: The pale neutral tone of this wall-to-wall Berber carpet blends into wall and window treatment to create the sense of a large flowing space. Wall-hugging furniture and built-ins with a few open-frame pieces ensures an uninterrupted visual flow, but the empty center actually gets plenty of informal use by the children in this family. The empty center also comes in handy for dinner parties and for moving the freestanding pieces when the sofa is opened up for overnight guests. A mirrored wall enlarges the living room area and joins it to the rest of the space. The Berber's looped pile does not take the imprint of vacuum strokes or footprints, and its random tweed pattern—which hides dirt, wear, and spills (as long as they are sponged up fairly quickly)—makes it ideal when a pale carpet is needed in a heavily trafficked area. Dining table and bookcase corners are rounded to create as much visual and physical space as possible in the narrowest part of the room.

where the natural moisture in soil or rock can affect them. Consequently, solid wood floors may not be the best choice in regions that have hot, humid summers followed by cold, dry winters, or in basements or the first floors of houses built on concrete slab.

Veneers are thin slices of flooring-quality wood laminated to plywood. Since the direction of the grain alternates in each ply, a veneer product is stronger and far less vulnerable to humidity. It is preferable for regions with extreme climate conditions, and can be used on or below grade and even in

kitchens. No wood product, however, can withstand the moisture conditions in bathrooms. The top layer of wood veneer is usually too thin to withstand more than one refinishing, and even then extreme care has to be exercised in the sanding to avoid cutting through to an inferior lower layer.

Wood borders are available in prefabricated sections that can be as simple or as elaborate as you want, or you can design your own. Borders can be used to formally delineate different functional areas within the same space or to encourage the eye to travel around the farthest reaches of a room.

FOLLOW THE BOUNCING COLORS

BELOW: Laying one carpet atop another does more than convince the eye that two rooms exist in this one small space; it also creates alternating blocks of light and dark that lead the eye step by step across the floor, up the wall, and out the window. The mauve wall-to-wall cut pile velvet is completely exposed in the dining area, it is covered by a black area rug in the living room, and it reemerges as a broad border at the far end of the floor. As the eye bounces through alternating bands of mauve and black it perceives floor, radiator cover, and window as one long plane; containing the color changes in large blocks lets the eye pause a bit on each to slow its progress through the space. To counteract the tunnel effect such a strong forward thrust can create, the different blocks of color are arranged to also pull the eye across the narrowest dimension of the room. A folding screen of mirrors widens the window wall, and mirrored walls broaden the dining area. Black lacquered columns between dining and sitting areas, large wall-hugging mauve sofas, and the pale horizontal blocks in the black rug reinforce the visual pull to the sides.

GRAY AREAS

ABOVE: A graphic-loop pile wall-to-wall carpet provides the crisp almost-tiled-floor look that these boldly modern furnishings seem to demand, but with more warmth and less cash outlay. Its medium neutral shade blends equally well with the black and the white pieces. The tiny sculpted repeat pattern subtly encourages the eye to keep moving around the room without coming to rest on any of the many densely solid objects. The carpet's recessive tone also pulls the floor a bit away from the ceiling, and shows less dirt than either black or white would.

Finishes

Prefinished wood has the stain and finish—usually some form of urethane—baked on in the factory. The initial purchase price is higher than for unfinished wood flooring, but tends to be offset by the labor costs—and time—that would be involved in finishing a floor on site. Prefinishes come in a limited variety of colors, however, and may darken with time.

Unfinished wood leaves the color entirely up to you. There are traditional wood stains, of course, or you can mix your own stain or use a colored product that lets the grain show through any number of decidedly non-wood shades—you can have a blue wood floor, a green wood floor, even a purple wood floor.

After an unfinished wood floor is laid, it must be sanded several times with increasingly finer grades of sandpaper, and then every speck of dust must be removed. The penetrating stain/sealer is applied to the floor in sections, allowed to sit for up to 15 minutes, then wiped clear and left to dry overnight. Flooring experts agree that, at this point, the best top finish is paste wax and a good buffing—but the rest of the population tends to disagree.

A paste wax finish, as elegant as it is, needs to be renewed and rebuffed every couple of weeks, and stripped and reapplied every few months. Scuffing is immediately apparent, and can easily go through to the wood surface. Liquid spills not wiped up immediately leave white marks that are difficult to remove. A wax finish works best in large institutions where there is a staff of knowledgeable cleaning help to keep up with the maintenance on a day-to-day basis.

In the average home, where it's next to impossible to find the time to maintain a wax finish on wood floors, hard polyurethane is the favorite. It is impervious to stains and watermarks, lasts for years depending on traffic, and doesn't look as "plastic" as it did in its early days. It tends to hide scuffs and keeps them from getting through to the wood itself. The low-gloss versions look the most like wax finishes and hide scuffs and dust the best.

DETAIL WITHOUT CLUTTER

BELOW: This oversize area rug is in the same pale color value as the walls, but the eye has to navigate a wood border in order to make the connection. The rug pattern keeps the eye moving around in the center of the floor, refusing to let the solid coffee table anchor it and pulling attention from the ceiling. Because the rug is a lighter value than the wood, the space between coffee table and wood border appears uncluttered. Positioning some of the leggy pieces of furniture half on the rug and half on the wood creates the illusion that the floor has no real beginning or end. The large, bright sofa does not overwhelm because its upholstery color is in the same family as the wood colors. Wood venetian blinds carry some floor tones up two walls; drawn half mast with slats slightly tilted, they minimize indifferent views while letting in plenty of light. A sense of the outdoors is also relayed by seascapes in recessive colors.

PATTERN SMOOTHS THINGS OUT

FACING PAGE: Pattern upon pattern can make an already small room appear claustrophobic, but here the addition of a large decorated dhurrie calms things down considerably. The rug's pileless construction and geometric pattern create a tile effect that organizes the space, anchors the extravagant patterning below eye level, and directs atten-

tion out to the perimeters of the room; the striations in the sectional upholstery follow the rug's direction. The rug's pink field and green accents contrast with the upholstery's yellows and oranges and create a slightly cooler, recessive foundation for the room. This is a tricky technique that may be difficult to pull off in a room where the other patterns don't have the layered qualities seen here.

WHITE OPEN SPACES

BELOW: This living/dining room is so small that any formal demarcation line between the eating and sitting areas would only call attention to how small each really is. However, a totally unpatterned high-gloss white marble floor permits the use of massive furniture elements—the thick dining table column, the black leather sectional—and lets *them* define each area. Glossy white also reflects maximum light, to create an illusion of expanding space; white

molding at the bottom of the walls makes the floor appear to extend even farther. The custom area rug introduces slight diagonals leading to a window that normally would not attract immediate attention. The corner column is dark to pull attention along the longest line of the room, but is mirrored to generate more light. The open-frame dining chairs let the floor flow through; their white seats minimize bulk.

A good polyurethane finish requires two coats, the first coat slightly abraded with fine steel wool so the next coat will adhere. The first coat usually needs overnight drying; the final coat may require more. Ordinary maintenance involves vacuuming, damp mopping, and an occasional application of a "conditioner" recommended by the polyurethane manufacturer; ordinary wood floor wax applied to polyurethane can create a greasy, slippery surface.

Before a polyurethane surface wears off completely, it can be renewed in high traffic spots by cleaning it thoroughly, roughing it up with fine steel wool, and reapplying the finish. If the protective surface has worn away to the wood and allowed the shade of the stain to change, the entire floor may have to be stripped and redone.

Painting and stenciling a basic wood floor can create charm as well as the illusion of more space. After a stencil pattern is completely dry, it should be protected with two coats of polyurethane, the first allowed to dry and then roughed up with fine steel wool before the final coat is applied.

Stenciling can be used to redirect attention by creating new lines that cut across the original line of the wood, or by a buildup of detail in corners. Bainbridge board is the best template material because it cleans easily and doesn't soften with use.

You can also paint an entire floor freehand, but steer clear of any form that people might feel disoriented stepping on—faces, for instance, or deep perspective scenes, water, clouds, or optical illusions that suggest a change in level.

WARM FLOOR FOR COOL EYE-LEVEL VIEW

ABOVE: Terrazzo, a composite product made of marble chips and concrete or epoxy, helps make this no-frills modern apartment appear to be located in a gracious older building. The pale tone helps pull the floor away from the low ceiling, while the hard surface makes for easy cleaning. Placing the Chinese rug at the angle of the L-shaped space formally separates the dining area, the living room, and the foyer without the use of view-stopping walls. Creamy natural raw-silk upholstery and natural wood frames keep the eye-level view of the room recessive and uncluttered. Even the massive sofa, placed dead center, and the armchair seem to disappear as the eye focuses on the warmer tones of the terrazzo, the carpet border, and the sunny ceiling-height valances. Terrazzo often seems warmer and more natural than marble, but just as elegant; the random organic shapes help to deemphasize grout lines where the tiles meet.

BROADENED HORIZON

FACING PAGE: Twelve-inch tiles of black marble with gray veining lend enough liveliness to this long, narrow room to keep it from looking like a museum—or, worse, a showroom—for cool, slick art furniture. To create a sense of continuing space, the marble is extended out to the terrace. The stripes of the hand-knotted woven area rug stretch the line of sight across the room's narrowest dimension, neatly deflecting attention from its length; the stripes lead to a separate seating area on one side and, on the other, a mirrored wall that appears to double the width of the room. The area rug rests on an open-mesh non-skid rubber pad cut five inches smaller than the rug on all sides to ease the transition from the pile surface to the marble.

SLEEK FLOOR FOILS FURNITURE MASS

ABOVE: This sleek marble tile floor deflects viewer attention from the fact that almost all the seats in this small room —including the dining chairs—are large and upholstered right down to floor. The only open-framed seat in the room is the one that is immediately visible from the entrance, as is the reflective planter. The use of small nine-inch tiles rather than the traditional twelve-inch version makes the room seem larger. A marble-block end table, tone-on-tone upholstery, and marble baseboards make the floor appear to continue upward into the vertical plane. The outdoor balcony becomes an extension of the room with the use of balancing greenery and with unpolished tiles of the same marble underfoot. Although the room's pale, monochromatic color scheme makes all the surfaces appear to recede, the result might have been bland without the richness of the marble floor.

THINKING GREEN

Some people believe that the use of wood in the home promotes the destruction of the rain forests, while others believe that, without a continuing profitable market for wood, the rain forests will be cut down anyway so the land can be used for other purposes. Some people believe it is safe to use wood from "farmed" forests, where every harvested tree is replaced with a new seedling, but others say that every time a mature tree is cut down an entire ecosystem disappears with it. The issues are tremendously complex and have given rise to entire books. One fact does seem to be clear, however: wood furnishings and flooring account for a small fraction of the trees that are cut down each year. The best idea—at least for now—may be to install a wood floor if that is your desire and at the same time become active in a group that addresses forest problems in a comprehensive fashion.

LEFT: Using carpet and marble tiles in the same room can do more than just mark off formal functions. Here, the floor treatment creates a border that defies the actual architecture of the space by making the far column a focal point of the dining room rather than its boundary marker, and pulling a mirrored section of wall out of the living room and into the dining room. This extra wedge of floor makes it possible to create a new center for the table, dictated by darker directional tiles, and to insert a seating area on the far side under the window. However, since the column has a mate at the edge of the near living room wall, the eye is still able to read the upper volume of the remapped wedge as belonging to the living room. The chain-patterned wall-to-wall carpet in the living room combines the same shades used in the dining room tiles and is laid diagonally to create diamonds that direct attention to both the length and the width of the room.

Carpeting

Broadloom carpet, the kind used for wall-to-wall installation, comes in wool, nylon, and a blend of the two; a 35-ounce broadloom should continue to look fine for eight to ten years.

Another option is sisal carpeting, made from plant fiber woven in strips broad enough for wall-to-wall installation.

Stain-resist treatments that are built into some carpeting at the time of manufacture may be worth the extra cost. Spray-on treatments, on the other hand, may discolor the fiber or kill the sheen on a fine wool cut pile; test the sprays on an inconspicuous spot—or try to get a sample piece of carpet from the manufacturer.

Underpadding lengthens the life and softens the feel of a wall-to-wall carpet, but it may buckle and cause you to have the whole carpet/pad combination restretched every few years. Underpadding should have a life expectancy equal to or better than the carpet that covers it; better to spend a bit more at the outset than to have to reinstall a perfectly good carpet because the pad underneath it has crumbled into dust. Carpet glued directly to the floor will never buckle but it will wear more quickly and not be as comfortable underfoot.

Carpet can make kitchen chores much less fatiguing, but stick to dense low-loop nylon (hot water causes drastic shrinkage in wool, and sisal not only shrinks but is too hard to clean) and a pattern that will hide ordinary dirt and wear. Just don't count on enlarging your space by using the same carpet in the kitchen and living/dining room, because different usage patterns will very quickly make the kitchen section look old and tired by comparison. Use a complimentary or contrasting carpet instead, or, if you must have a match, use vinyl or ceramic tile in the kitchen in the same shade as the living/dining room carpet. Bathrooms also can be carpeted but, again, keep away from wool and sisal.

Fiber Content

Wool wears longest, holds color best, responds best to wet cleaning methods, and looks and feels better than any other kind of carpeting. It usually has a lovely sheen.

Nylon is less expensive and more stain resistant than wool, but harder to clean once a stain takes hold. High-end nylons can look and feel as good as wool. A cheap nylon carpet will have a bit of a hard shine (not to be confused with the soft sheen of wool).

Blends come in several combinations, but 80 percent wool and 20 percent nylon seems to produce the best combination of both fibers.

Sisal is extremely durable and takes color well, but it stains easily and is difficult to clean. Sisal does not hide its seams well and should be used only where the directional line aids the overall design. Since it has a tendency to shrink, sisal may not be suitable for tight wall-to-wall installations in humid climates. Walking on pure sisal's rough surface without shoes could possibly run nylons; children tumbling around on it could develop friction burns. Sisal/wool blends tend to be softer.

Textures

Looped pile is the most durable because any pressure that's put on it is distributed through a springy curve. It is best for patterns, since the low-pile loop bounces back upright. Looped pile may remind some people of commercial carpet, but traditional needlepoint designs also fall into this category.

Berber has a larger, thicker loop. Contrary to popular opinion, it is not limited to natural tones, although the loop is too floppy to be used successfully in multicolor patterns.

Cut pile has a lush velvety texture that tends to highlight footprints and vacuum cleaner strokes. The higher the pile and the looser the density, the more obvious these marks will be.

Combined cut/looped piles are used to create patterns in broadloom carpeting.

Area Rugs

Area carpets run the gamut from pure silk prayer rugs to stitched lengths of braided rags, and can be used to grab attention, turn the eye in a new direction, or lead the eye along a winding route composed of small or moderate-size objects of the same color.

An underpad is necessary to keep an area rug from skidding on a hard floor but, since it adds to the height of the rug, it can also increase the chance of tripping. To create a more graduated effect, cut a thin rubber mesh pad two inches smaller than the rug on all sides; if you prefer a thicker pad, cut it four to five inches smaller than the rug on all sides. Avoid spray-on slip-resist treatments: they can harm the fiber and break down the construction of the rug.

Other Flooring Possibilities

Cork is a naturally springy material some people like in the kitchen because it is easy on the feet. But it stains easily, even with pretreatment, and is difficult to maintain.

Rubber, which is available in heavy interlocking mats ranging from $3/8$ inch to $1/2$ inch thick, comes in a variety of colors and patterns. It is also easy on your feet, but its tendency to dry out and develop a cloudy surface makes maintenance somewhat complex.

Leather is gorgeous but expensive and requires a great deal of polishing. If you are not completely convinced that naturally occurring scratches and discolorations are part of the mellow beauty of a floor, don't buy leather.

ORGANIZING THE ECCENTRIC

ABOVE: The custom furnishings in this small room are all strikingly angled for two reasons. Some, like the sofa, hug the wall and cut corners in order to save space, and others are art furniture that the owner wants to display—note the dining table pulled out at an angle to show off its jagged edge and the noses and ears carved into its columnar base. Black ceramic tiles laid in a foursquare pattern make a perfect foil for the display, and also impose a sense of direction to militate against any sense of disori-entation or claustrophobia that such an eccentric collection of angles might otherwise cause. Since the table is so dramatic, no change in flooring is needed to delineate the dining area from the living room. The small size of the eight-inch tiles means more tiles are used, leading to the impression that the floor is larger than it is; the subtle cloud pattern lends an organic feel in an otherwise slick room. Since they have a non-slip surface, they were used, along with the tall foliage indoors and out, to carry the room out onto the balcony.

Walls

All our indoor spaces are essentially boxes. How we cover and color the interior surfaces greatly determines how large these rooms will appear and how comfortable we feel in them—whether we feel we can breathe, stretch, and stride, or whether we feel confined and restricted.

The two most common finishes for walls are paint and wallpaper. Between them, they provide an enormous range of color, texture, and finish that combine to create any number of space-enhancing optical illusions.

However, there is also a third material that designers rely on extensively, but that most householders still seem to approach with too much timidity—the mirror, which can cover entire walls to create an illusion of more than double the existing space or, in smaller doses, simply let some light and air into tight corners.

THE OLD STANDBY: PAINT

A simple coat of paint is the easiest and least expensive way to cover a wall, and the quickest to correct if the results are not quite what you expected.

If it's been a while since you've done any painting, some of your assumptions about the material may be obsolete. Advances in technology have all but eliminated the old tendency of high-gloss paints to chip more than flat ones, and water-based paints now cling as well as oil-based. Talk to the salespeople in a good paint store; they can give you free literature, sell you inexpensive booklets on technique, and get you how-to videos from the manufacturers.

When chosen in the proper hues and finishes, paint can influence the perception of space:

- Dark and warm-toned surfaces seem to approach, while light and cool ones seem to retreat or even disappear. For instance, a ceiling in a lighter or cooler tone than the walls will appear higher than it really is, while a darker or warmer color will lower the ceiling and seem to push out the walls beneath. In a long, narrow room, a darker or warmer color on the end walls will seem to pull them closer and push paler or cooler side walls farther apart.
- Dark and warm-toned walls can create wonderful sensations of drama or intimacy, but other space-making details must be introduced to counteract the tendency of a dark room to shrink. Almost every hint in this book can help open the space up again, but study the chapter on lighting with special care.

- Gloss imparts a sense of coolness to a surface, while matte finishes appear warmer and more enveloping.
- When walls match carpeting or upholstery (just bring a sample to a paint store and the computer does the rest), the combination reads as one expansive surface rather than two or more smaller ones.
- Since each texture reflects light in its own way, a variety of surfaces in the same color may not appear to match perfectly. However, the total design of a room—and especially its lighting—focuses attention on a number of elements, and any discrepancy will be noticeable only to someone who's deliberately looking for it. On color chips, the exact same color will appear somewhat different, depending on varying degrees of shine, but in a completed room the eye will read gloss-covered metal or wood as a match for flat-covered plaster or drywall.
- A completely monotone room can make you feel as though the walls are closing in, but subtle gradations of the same color—one for the walls, a bit lighter for the ceiling, a bit darker for trim, and so on through flooring, furnishings, and window treatments—can give the space the same feeling of depth that shadow and light give to a painting.
- Shelves and cabinets will tend to disappear when covered with the same tone as the surrounding walls; conversely, window frames painted in a contrasting color will call attention to a room-expanding view.
- Although bold colors at eye level can make a room seem smaller, the same colors used up, down, and around an area can encourage the eye to travel, actually increasing the illusion of space.
- Touches of unexpected color that draw the eye can also stop it cold at that point unless there is something interesting farther on—for example, a colorful molding at the edge of a plain, flat ceiling initially draws the eye upward, but if there is a lighting cove or some fanciful plaster work or a mural of clouds farther on, the eye will continue its journey. (Be wary of bold trim, however, in a room where structural columns, odd angles, mismatched windows, or too many doorways interfere with the sense of an unbroken flow of space.)

PAINT FINISHES

Most paints come in a choice of four finishes, flat and three gradations of gloss: satin (also known as soft gloss), semigloss, and high gloss. Some paint companies also offer three more finish grades—eggshell, low-luster, and pearl—which fit in the spectrum between flat and satin. As the names imply, they provide a subtle degree of glow rather than a shine.

Flat

Advantages: Flat (or matte) finishes reflect the least light back to the eye and spare us from knowledge we'd rather not have about imperfections in the surface—bumps, bulges, cracks, chips, overlooked nail holes, old alligatored paint, discrepancies between old and new plaster, and the different textures that result from rolling and brushing.

Disadvantages: Flatter paints tend to absorb dirt and don't stand up well to the scrubbing needed to clean the surface.

Gloss

Advantages: The shinier the surface, the less likely it is to absorb dirt and stains, the easier it is to wipe off, and the better it will stand up to scrubbing.

Disadvantages: The shinier the surface, the more light it reflects back to our eyes, and the more noticeable the imperfections will appear. Creating an absolutely smooth expanse of wall is usually a job for professionals and can be quite expensive.

To achieve the best compromise between flat and gloss, most people opt for semigloss, but the even less glossy paint finishes may better suit your purposes. A paint store should be able to give you manufacturer's paint chips showing all your options.

DRAMATIC DISAPPEARANCE

ABOVE: No matter how often we see it, no matter how safe landlords and developers and timid people think it is, white remains one of the most visually stunning colors for walls. The lightest possible of all shades, it has the greatest ability to disappear—without losing any of its drama.

In this 500-square-foot studio, all the virtues of white are magnified in a custom glaze of oil paint and joint compound applied in eight thin layers on walls as smooth as it is possible to make them. The final effect is a mirrorlike surface that more than doubles the amount of perceived space in the room. White floors and furnishings tend to dissolve into the space, while vivid touches of color in the owner's art collec-

tion and in some throw pillows draw the eye to distant parts.

Other space-expanding techniques include a mirrored wall above the built-in day bed, a mirrored structural column between the banks of windows, radiator covers expanded to accommodate bookcases, floor tiles and an area rug laid on the diagonal, see-through glass tops on coffee and dining tables, and open-frame side chairs that let light pass right through them. Recessed spotlights in the ceiling over the white sculpture prevent the art from disappearing into the background the way the white dining chairs do. The black-bordered zebra rug anchors the space (this much white could float away like a cloud), defines the seating area, and establishes a walkway toward the dining area.

CARPET COLOR REPEATED ON WALLS

FACING PAGE: This living room area is not much longer or wider than the sectional seating along its perimeters, but the illusion of more space is created by continuing the soft tones of the carpet in the flat latex paint on the walls and room-dividing entertainment unit. A slightly deeper tone of the same color is used for the upholstery. The ceiling is a soft off-white. Other space-expanding techniques include a vibrant painting and contrasting pillows to draw the eye to

the farthest reaches; rounded corners on the divider cabinet; an art panel of etched glass that permits a free flow of light; a torchère that lifts the ceiling with a soft pool of light; and translucent pleated shades lowered halfway to extend the boundaries of the room without celebrating the confining view of other buildings. While the extensive use of a single color expands the room, it is the judicious touches of another color, in this case green, that tie the design together.

WHERE TO USE WHAT PAINT

- Glossier finishes are best for surfaces that suffer a lot of friction or require regular cleaning: kitchens, bathrooms, handrails, door and window trim, bookshelves, narrow halls and stairways, and almost any place frequented by children.
- Oil-based paints and alkyds are the best choices for bathrooms and kitchens, constantly touched surfaces such as doors, and households that tend to put off repainting for long stretches of time.
- Latex is best for walls and ceilings in bedrooms, living rooms, and formal dining rooms, and for households that enjoy frequent color-scheme changes.
- Latex is ideal if you need to see the whole room painted before making up your mind. If the problem room ultimately will need an oil-based or alkyd paint, experiment with latex to find the perfect colors, and then recoat with the more durable paint. Latex is the easiest for experiments with faux finishes, too.
- Surface defects are more apparent on a ceiling than on a wall—use flat finishes on ceilings.
- The eye accepts—and expects—metal and wood in the same or glossier finishes than the surrounding plaster or drywall, but flatter trim accompanying a glossier wall can feel confusing.
- Use primer/sealers, especially when painting a light color over a dark one or applying any paint over a high-gloss finish.
- Don't count on good results from bargain-basement or over-thinned paints.

PAINT COMPOSITION

Every finish and color imaginable are available in both water-based and oil-base paints.

Latex Paints

Water-based latex paints are the most popular and easiest to use, but the least durable.

Advantages: Quick drying; mild odor; can be easily recoated with oil-based or alkyd paints; brushes and rollers clean up with soap and water.

Disadvantages: Less durable and less water resistant than oil-based paints; stand up less well to scrubbing.

Oil-Based and Alkyd Paints

Relatively difficult to work with, oil-based paints and their modern equivalent, alkyd paints, are nevertheless the most durable and moisture resistant.

Advantages: Durable; washable; moisture resistant; best for overcoats of varnish or tinted polyurethane.

Disadvantages: Longer drying time than latex; brush and roller cleanup requires solvents *plus* soap and water; strong odor; requires a primer sealer before latex can be applied over it.

Anti-Allergy, Ecologically Friendly Paints

People who are allergic to oil-based and/or latex paints may want to investigate "natural" paints that cause little or no reaction during painting or drying. However, conditions for storage, mixing, and drying tend to be very exacting, and if something goes wrong, over time the surface itself can become a host to fungi and other allergens.

The topic requires research that goes far beyond the scope of this book, but the paint store, the library, and your allergist or the allergy department of your local teaching hospital are good places to start.

FAUX FINISHES

Glazing, washing, rubbing, stippling, spattering, sponging, combing, or rag rolling a second color —or third or fourth—over the first can add a subtle suggestion of depth to a painted wall, while marbleizing and wood-graining can add a look of luxury.

Faux finishes are not nearly so simple as slapping on a coat of paint, but are far more fun to do if you've got the time and enjoy experimenting. Any lumberyard will be happy to cut you manageable pieces of drywall at decent prices so you can experiment all you want without defacing your actual walls. As you experiment, jot down the formula for each new color or dilution you create so that you can re-create batch after batch of the ones you like best.

Whatever you do, don't worry that a faux finish will look like a cheap imitation: most of them don't copy anything found in nature, and earlier in this century *faux marbre* was considered so distinguished that designers used marbleized paint finishes over the real thing!

Faux finishing involves applying layers of paint— latex over latex, oil over oil, oil over latex (but generally not latex over oil) in patterns ranging from soft to bold, and using a variety of tools, some of them rather surprising. Acrylic paints, which mimic oils but are less toxic, are more difficult to work with because they dry more quickly. Before applying faux finishes, use a primer to seal old paint on plaster or drywall; wood surfaces should be unfinished or stripped down to raw, and sealed.

For most of the effects, the second coat should be darker than the first and in the same family of hues; as anyone who has ever played with a paint box knows, contrasting colors tend to blend into a muddy brown.

Major Faux Finishes

Color Wash

A color wash is a simple wash of translucent color over a white base coat. Dilute the color coat with three to four times as much of the appropriate thinner and brush on. Wipe off the excess with a rag or sponge, or work it out with brushstrokes. The effect is subtly textured and on the matte side.

Scrubbing

Sometimes called rubbing, scrubbing is dragging the second coat on with a "dry brush"—that is, one that is moistened with paint but not fully loaded; it should leave a brush texture on the surface. This technique works best with an eggshell-finish oil paint as the first coat, and a latex as the second. As soon as the latex is dry—in an hour or two—rub it with denatured alcohol to achieve more texture and reveal more of the first coat. The effect is a little distressed and uneven.

Oil Glaze

Products called oil glazes or glazing liquids, which can be purchased at paint stores and tinted with oil colors out of tubes purchased at art supply stores, are used for a second coat. Start with the least amount of tint and experiment until you get the shade of glaze that you need. Apply with one brush, and blend and feather with a second, clean brush. The glaze can also be wiped while it is wet. Glazing makes every surface look richer and more refined. Oil glazing can be taken a few steps further by using one of the following techniques:

Stippling—gently pounding the tip of a stiff, flat-edged paintbrush into the wet glaze to create a subtle speckled effect. Stippling brushes from art supply stores can be expensive; short-bristled flat-edged

SPATTER EFFECT FOR DEPTH

FACING PAGE: A fine spatter of a slightly lighter shade covers the first coat of paint on the walls, radiator covers, structural columns, and soffits of this small, narrow studio. The two-toned effect gives the impression that the room extends slightly beyond its immediate surfaces. The oyster background and white spatters are latex.

Other space-expanding techniques include lengthening the radiator cover to create bookcases; open-framed bistro and coffee tables (the latter glass-topped); and an expanse of upholstery striped to carry the eye across (and therefore stretch) the room's narrowest dimension.

brushes from the hardware store do the job just as well, though it will take a bit longer.

Ragging—pounding a scrunched-up cloth into the glaze to create an irregular faceted texture. When the rag stops making patterns, scrunch up a clean one and keep going. When the glaze has dried for about half an hour, it is possible to go over it with a brush to soften the broken lines for a more mottled effect. The best rags for ragging are clean, lint-free, 100 percent cotton or linen with all buttons, hems, seams, and decorative stitching removed. Although synthetic and blended fabrics don't work well, scrunched-up plastic bags can, but they have to be replaced frequently and don't provide the most refined surfaces.

Strié—dragging a long-haired brush or a special "flogging" brush vertically through an oil glaze. The brush has to be dragged downward in one continuous motion in order to pull the glaze into soft vertical lines for a formal, non-random effect.

Combing—drawing metal or rubber combs, available in a variety of sizes from art supply and specialized paint stores, through an oil glaze. The combs can be drawn in curves, waves, semicircles, S shapes, or figure eights, or can be used to mimic wood grain. The effect can be Early American folk art or even stylized Japanese.

Spatter

Spatter is probably the messiest of the faux finishes, since the technique involves flicking wet paint off the end of a brush onto a wall to create layers of opaque dots. The brush is fully loaded, with the excess flicked off into the can, and then flicked against a stick held about a foot away from the wall (use a toothbrush instead of a paintbrush for small areas). Spatter requires some practice, since the closer to the wall and the more forceful the flick, the larger the dots are likely to be; the longer the brush bristles, the larger the area the flick will cover. As each color dries, another layer of colored dots can be added; do some experiments before deciding on color combinations and number of layers. Black or gold spatter on red can create an Oriental effect; a variety of natural tones can produce a stonelike finish.

Wood Grain and Marbleizing

Brushes, combs, rockers (like rubber stamps with wood-grain patterns), veining brushes, and even feathers are used to create effects with paint. The technique is more similar to art than to house painting. When the results are convincing the effect is amazing, but when they are not convincing the effect can be appalling. Classes in these techniques may be offered at a community college, art school, or even a paint store, but if your time is money, it may be cheaper in the long run to hire a professional.

The methods discussed above are meant to be only a starting point. Possibilities for faux finishes are limited only by your imagination. You could, for instance, break the rules for ragging and use embroidered fabric or lace to create a whole new texture. You could experiment with pressing window screening into a glaze, or ice-cube trays with tiny compartments, or Harris tweeds, or spinach leaves, or your hands and feet. Try out different color combinations to create a leather look. Use a wash to paint ethereal patterns. You could do almost anything you want, and in the process perhaps discover a look you weren't expecting but wind up loving.

Whatever faux finish you choose, look for instruction booklets and manufacturers' videos at your paint store, and entire books devoted to the techniques at your library or bookstore. Whether you do the job yourself or hire a professional, a faux finish is a major investment. Don't forget to protect it with a final coat of polyurethane or varnish.

A FEELING OF ALL OUTDOORS

FACING PAGE: A hand-painted faux stone wall behind the bed turns an awkward arrangement of structural column and beam into a shallow niche that, by mimicking the outdoors, suggests more depth than actually exists. Irregular patterns like fieldstone or rough-hewn granite could benefit from less-than-perfect subsurface textures, but smooth-cut patterns like this one would look more phoney than faux if defective wall surfaces were to show through. Other space-expanding techniques involve sconce light to draw the eye into the alcove and seemingly raise the semigloss ceiling over the bed; a subtle pattern of dots in the carpet that matches the "stone" color and directs attention toward the illusory alcove; curved cabinetry to open up passages; matching bed frame and tailored cover; mirrored doors on the headboard storage unit; and a gathering of drapery to conceal a structural column and make the windows seem to extend across the entire wall.

A TINY BIT OF GLOW

BELOW: Glowing phosphoric blue stenciled motifs strategically placed above the bed create a focal point without breaking up the only large stretch of wall in this compact bedroom. The placement of the designs, their vertical thrust, and their upward curves all add a bit of extra height to the walls, and distract from the more densely packed opposite side of the room. The phosphoric paint, Bainbridge board, and mat knives used to create the stencil motif are available at reasonable prices from art supply stores. The wall itself is olive latex spattered with off-white, a darkish combination that emphasizes the view.

Other space-expanding techniques here are the use of black to make the radiator covers and dust ruffles seem to disappear, and white to turn the fluffy comforter into an airy expanse.

BEDCOVER AS CUE

FACING PAGE: A sponged latex pattern blends all the colors found throughout this bedroom into pale, cloudlike forms that seem to float beyond the boundaries of the wall. A thin cornice of crown molding (available at lumberyards in a wide variety of shapes and sizes) colored with an oil-based paint visually anchors the walls and eases the transition to the tan ceiling. The ceiling color has the same value as the colors in the carpet and furniture, which seems to push the paler walls farther away.

The entire color scheme for this room deliberately takes its cue from the inexpensive bedcover. While it is always possible to find a wide selection of paints, carpets, and upholsteries that will work with your favorite bedcover, bedcover selections are so limited that finding a match after the room is designed is next to impossible.

A MILLION AND ONE POSSIBILITIES: WALLCOVERINGS

Often referred to as wallpaper, contemporary wallcoverings go well beyond papers to include easy-care vinyls, reflective metallics, and even fabrics.

An easy way to introduce texture into a room, wallcoverings are also an effective means of increasing the feeling of space. Strong vertical patterns will make ceilings seem higher, while designs with predominantly horizontal lines will make walls seem wider. A patterned wallcovering used in an alcove will draw the eye into its depths; on a single wall it will distract the eye from other boundaries. Extending a wallpaper pattern into the ceiling will increase the sense of space (this is a job for a professional).

Border patterns are available for use with wallcoverings or as trim on painted walls. Used at chair-rail height (24 to 30 inches above the floor), they can broaden a room. Used along the ceiling, they can make a plain wall seem taller, but unless they have a strong vertical pattern they may call a halt to the heightening effects of a vertically patterned wall.

As with paint, lighter colors tend to make rooms seem larger, while richer, darker colors help create more intimacy or drama and require greater attention to other design elements, especially lighting. And, as with painted faux finishes, layered patterns and embossed patterns impart a subtle depth to a wall.

Specialty wallcoverings like foils, mylars, and metallics create space-expanding mirror effects, but since they exaggerate even the smallest irregularity in wall surfaces, meticulous preparatory work is especially important. On the other hand, such specialties as embossed and flocked wallcoverings may help to disguise less than perfect walls.

Fabric wallcoverings can continue the flow of draperies, bed linens, or upholstery around the room to expand the sense of space, and also help soundproof the room. If treated with fabric protector, these wallcoverings will remain fresh for long periods of time, but keep in mind that wall-hung fabric that is rarely touched will age differently from constantly handled fabric used on a bed or upholstered furniture.

A WALL BEHIND THE WALL

LEFT: The crackled pattern in this matte-finish vinyl wallcovering makes it appear that the real wall is somewhere behind an airy grille of delicate twigs. The intricate pattern is a deft camouflage for imperfections in the wall surface.

Other space-expanding techniques include the low placement of bulky stereo equipment on a ledge finished in the same paper as the wall, glass shelves that appear to float in cool blue neon light, and a torchère that calls attention to the upper reaches of the walls.

MORE SPACE IN THE WINGS

ABOVE: Vertical bands of horizontally striated embossed vinyl wallcovering draw the eye both upward *and* outward at the end of this narrow space. To reinforce the sense of height, the wallcovering continues over the baseboard molding; the upper molding is painted a stark white to draw the eye upward and lift the ceiling away from the wall. The far end of this room is really the terminus of a hallway, which the use of ceiling molding gathers firmly into the room; beneath the molding, however, the wallcovering extends into the rest of the hallway to reinforce the sense of continuous space. The uniform pattern of this wallcovering makes it unsuitable for disguising imperfections in the wall underneath.

HANGING FABRIC

Fabric can be mounted directly on a plywood panel or to the wall itself using spray or roll-on glues available in art supply stores. Keep in mind that some kind of framing effect is inevitable, since molding will be needed to cover the seams—unlike papers, the cut edges of fabric tend to stretch and ravel and make pattern-matching a nightmare. Furthermore, direct gluing cannot be used with silks or thin fabrics that expose flaws in the wall surface, the grain of the plywood panel, and even the texture of the glue itself.

The best method of hanging fabric involves wrapping it around a foam-covered plywood panel not quite as wide as the fabric and stapling it to the back; if you tell your hardware store what you're up to, they will be able to sell you the proper hardware for hanging your upholstered panel on the wall. Clearly, the upholstered panel will bring the wall forward up to an inch into the room, but still there are some advantages: hemmed fabric can be removed with a staple remover and washed or dry cleaned; fabric is a great cover-up if you find yourself stuck with truly bad plaster work (as, for instance, when a landlord refuses to invest in repairs); and if you use rare or expensive fabric, you just remove the frame from the wall and take it with you when you move.

DIAMONDS GO THE DISTANCE

LEFT: The paper wallcovering in this rather small bedroom relies on a diamond pattern to visually raise the ceiling. Soft pastel shadings create intimacy without overwhelming. Latex eggshell ceiling paint matches the wallcovering's lighter shade of pink and creates the space-enhancing illusion of a continuous wall-ceiling surface. The wallcovering's regular pattern will not effectively hide irregularities in the surface beneath.

Other space-expanding techniques involve a tailored bedcovering and matching frame that echo the diagonal thrust of the wallcovering; a matte natural laminate finish on the cabinetry; a free-floating vanity; chamfered cabinetry corners to create easy passages; subtle vertical stripes in curtains that rise all the way to the ceiling; and a plain round mirror that acts as a large porthole to extend the view of the room.

UPWARD BOUND

FACING PAGE: A vinyl-backed moiré-patterned paper directs the eye up the walls of this bedroom and suggests the depths of shimmering water. The ceiling is a pale blue. In this serene sea-sky scheme, the bold headboard in a totally unexpected color further directs the eye upward.

Other space-expanding techniques involve a mirror-covered dresser that almost disappears as it reflects and extends the carpet; micro-venetian blinds extended beyond the window frame to cover the shallow structural column at left; and high-gloss black cabinetry that recedes into the background as it pivots around a corner to form a shallow desk below the window. A surprising swath of pale blue under the desk draws attention to the window and seems to give it added length.

BEFORE YOU CHOOSE

Try not to fall in love with a wallpaper before you study the imperfections in your walls and learn how much you will have to invest to replaster or replace them with wallboard. It might be wiser to compromise on a camouflaging wallcovering and use the savings on the other design elements in the space. Here are some options:

• Vinyl-backed papers don't wrinkle and can help hide some deficiencies in the underlying wall.
• Intricate and bold patterns distract attention from problem walls; regular geometrics can call attention to problems.
• Pretrimmed wallpapers may sound easier to use, but if your walls are not perfect you may want to have the extra leeway that selvage provides.
• Thin vinyls show surface imperfections, and thick vinyls tend to hide them.

There are other important factors to consider before making your final decisions:

• Lightweight papers have a tendency to tear, and should be hung by professionals.
• Wallpapers protected by a thin plastic coating are washable but *not* scrubbable.
• Vinyl wallpapers are both washable *and* scrubbable, and are therefore ideal for kitchens, bathrooms, playrooms, and any other space that takes repeated abuse.
• Wallcovering marked "strippable" can be completely removed from the wall at redecorating time without steaming or scraping. "Peelable" coverings permit the coated top layer to be peeled away so that solvent can get through to the paper backing.
• Special cleaners to clean embossed and flocked styles are available from wallcovering stores.

GRID SMOOTHS OVER IRREGULARITIES

ABOVE: A graphic grid-patterned wallpaper, coated with a plastic finish for easy maintenance, covers the upper three quarters of these walls. The wallpaper gives the impression of sky seen through a lattice (the blue carries through into the matte ceiling) and lends some regularity to a room whose structural oddities call attention to its small size. Mirror-covered structural columns create an infinite repeat of the grid pattern. On the bottom portion of the wall, a dado and chair rail painted in a coordinating color sweep directly into the matching below-window cabinetry; a new coat of paint on the dado and chair rail can refresh the room without requiring an entire repapering.

Other space-expanding techniques involve mirrored cabinet tops, which reflect light and make the windows look larger; a transparent tabletop and open-framed chairs; wall-mounted light fixtures that seem to hover in midair; and what must be the world's tiniest nightstand—a simple plate glass shelf slipped through a custom slot in the drywall and anchored to a stud with silicone glue.

THE WALL UNDER THE PAPER

Heavy-duty liners are available that can create a smooth surface even over the pits of concrete block and the recesses of its grout. Unfortunately, while these liners work miracles with wallcoverings, they will not accept paint. Nor will they do much for big, ominous bulges in the wall, which, if not confronted now, could hatch into repair jobs that will be twice as difficult—and expensive—as doing the job right the first time. And while anyone can spackle a nail hole, a dent, or a hairline crack, for large patchy areas, surfaces that wave in and out, and recurring cracks, most of us need professionals—they have the skills and tricks and years of experience necessary to create smoothness in problem areas.

THROUGH THE LOOKING GLASS: MIRRORS

Quite simply, mirrors make boundaries disappear. Not only does a mirror reflect—that is, double—everything in its vicinity, it also seems to have no substance of its own. It convinces us, as it did Alice, that there is room for another world behind it.

Used generously or with restraint, mirrors yield the most dramatic space-expanding results. Entire walls can be covered in sheets up to six feet by ten feet, which requires professional installation, or in smaller do-it-yourself tiles. If an entire wall seems a bit over-whelming, a strategically placed mirrored folding screen or a mirrored column, border, alcove, or book-case interior can still create a substantial increase in perceived space. So, for that matter, can old-fashioned hanging mirrors, with or without frames.

Advantages: Mirrors add sparkle as well as the illusion of expanded space. They can last for thirty years, with easy cleaning and no upkeep.

Disadvantages: Small mirror tiles need smooth, plumb walls in order to butt properly. Mirrors show signs of food frying and cigarette smoking more quickly than any other surfacing material.

MIRRORED SCREEN

ABOVE: The subtle use of mirrors increases the perceived size of this small bedroom by opening up the dead space be-tween the bed and a structural column. The column itself is mirrored, and a mirrored three-panel, floor-to-ceiling fold-ing screen is positioned in front to bring in multi-angled views of the skyline. A framed mirror in the middle of the opposite wall balances the effect.

Other space-expanding techniques involve the use of black to make the wraparound cabinetry and carpeting recede; continuation of the wall color into the ceiling; a simple but dramatic black Roman shade that directs the eye to the view out the window; and coordinated uphol-stery and bed coverings that draw the eye on a diagonal from the bed to the chaise.

LEARNING TO USE MIRRORS

- Don't install a mirror just for the sake of installing one. Experiment with a large hanging mirror or a piece of Mylar to find the best placement for the effects you need. Look into it from every possible angle to make sure it doesn't reflect something you'd just as soon not have two of.
- Place mirrors opposite or at a 90-degree angle to windows to multiply the amount of daylight in a room, bring the outside world in, and make it seem as if you have far more windows than you actually do.
- Use mirrors on the same wall as windows to extend the windowlike feeling without reflecting the view.
- Place a mirrored shelf or cabinet top beneath a window to make the window appear longer by as many feet as the mirrored surface is deep.
- Angle mirrors into corners to capture a wide sweep of reflections and create a smooth transition from one wall to another.
- Use floor-to-ceiling mirrors to double the perceived size of a room, but be careful to place low pieces of furniture in front of large unbroken expanses of mirror to make sure no one is tempted to walk into the illusory space.
- Install mirrors on facing walls to create repeating reflections with an illusion of infinite space; again, arrange low pieces of furniture up against the mirrored surface to prevent disorientation.
- Mirror the backsplashes in kitchen and bathroom, and the wall surfaces between upper and lower cabinets in bedrooms and home offices, to create the illusion of additional space and to make wall-hung cabinetry appear to float.
- Use strips of mirror along the tops of walls to make the ceiling float. (Don't use a strip of mirror close to the floor, however, for it could give the unnerving impression that the walls have no base and could come crashing down.)
- Try color. A peach-tinted mirror adds warmth and a flattering glow to bedrooms or dressing rooms (but don't depend on it for applying makeup). Bronze or black can add drama to a formal dining or living room.
- To attach art, lighting fixtures, or even framed mirrors to a mirrored wall, drill holes before the mirror is installed or use glue-on clips.
- Cover a wall with a variety of mirrors in interesting frames.
- Use double-faced adhesive tape to install moldings or chair rails on a mirrored surface.
- To create an extra window exactly where you want it, use mirrored tiles with narrow molding between the tiles, and a wider molding as a border. (Despite the increasing prevalence of large single-pane windows in the real world, our minds still seem to think window means mullions, and will not accept a faux window without them.)
- Don't buy a large mirror without first checking that it will fit in your elevator and through your doors and halls.
- Don't be put off by patterns in mirrors or even the recurring lines between do-it-yourself tiles. The point in using a mirrored surface is not to achieve a precise mirror image but to obtain the illusion of *more*: more space, more light, more psychological breathing room.

THREE-WAY EXPANSION

FACING PAGE: Mirrored surfaces expand this room in three different directions. A floor-to-ceiling mirror on the same plane as the window extends the sense of windowlike openness and helps to double the perceived size of the room; a painted chair rail protects the mirror. At a right angle to the window, beveled mirror tiles cover the lower wall to double both the room and the view, and to lend a sense of weightlessness to the wall-hung storage cabinets. At far right, mirrors cover the bi-fold doors, reducing the apparent bulk of the closet space. The bed is edged in reflecting chrome tubing.

Other space-expanding techniques involve indirect lighting above the wall-hung storage cabinets to lift the ceiling; a simple uplight sconce on the mirrored window wall to draw attention to the ceiling; extending the protective chair rail into a decorative edge for the desk; angled placement of the bed to further distract from the confining walls; the airy columns on the bed base, which add depth and vertical thrust; the use of sharp accent colors (like the bright red for the chair) to draw the eye out to the farthest boundaries of the room; and waist-high planters/storage units that define an edge for the room without closing it off.

HIDDEN DEPTHS

ABOVE: A wall of mirrors not only doubles the apparent size of this room but also hides a wealth of storage. A double-imaged torchère raises the ceiling in what now appears to be the center of the space (but is actually the edge), while a recessed ceiling lamp and a lower reading lamp glowing against the drapes draw the eye as far as possible into the reflected room.

Other space-expanding techniques involve upholstered armless dining chairs that appear substantial but not bulky, and glass-topped open-framed tables that permit the view to flow right through them.

CHANGING PROPORTIONS

FACING PAGE: Instead of a mirrored wall, this bedroom features three mirrored panels separated by painted vertical moldings. The moldings echo the three dressers below and draw the eye upward from the horizontal flow of hardware. The glow from a triangular sconce mounted on the mirror lifts the ceiling. Since the mirrors make the room appear extra long, cabinetry, hardware, and bedcover stripes flow across what now appears to be the room's narrowest dimension. The walls and ceiling are both covered in the same flat off-white paint.

THE ILLUSION OF BALANCE

ABOVE: A full mirrored wall not only doubles the perceived space in this dining/living room but turns the impossibly located structural column into a surprising asset. The window is reflected in the mirror and gives the impression of two. The mirrored reflections also make the column appear to be more centrally located and therefore a good focal point for the display of art. Other space-expanding techniques involve the use of clear white paint and crisp white tiles on the floor to give an airy feeling. Black window frames echo the floor grid pattern.

INFINITE SPACE

FACING PAGE: Mirroring opposing walls creates an infinity of reflections within reflections, as shown in this small living/dining room. Mirrored structural columns and portions of the window wall reinforce the multiplicity of images and illusions of space, while wall-hugging furniture arrangements prevent disorientation. A polished metal base for the dining table and polished metal inserts between the coffee-table top and its legs introduce some air.

Other space-expanding techniques involve an expanse of white carpet; built-in dining banquettes; and shoji-screen panels that permit daylight to enter while concealing an ugly view (there is nothing that blocks the flow of vision like ugliness). At night, recessed downlights directed on the screens give them a daylight glow that hints at outdoor spaces. The accompanying drawings show how to create the illusion of space on the upper walls while carving out real space for storage below.

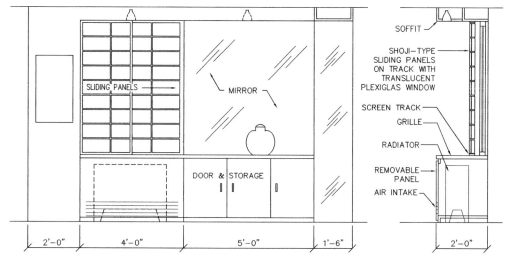

SOFFIT

SHOJI–TYPE
SLIDING PANELS
ON TRACK WITH
TRANSLUCENT
PLEXIGLAS WINDOW

SCREEN TRACK

GRILLE

RADIATOR

REMOVABLE
PANEL

AIR INTAKE

SLIDING PANELS

MIRROR

DOOR & STORAGE

2'-0"   4'-0"   5'-0"   1'-6"   2'-0"

Elevation   Section

Window Wall Treatment

POLISHED STONE

ABOVE: This room makes a dramatic break from the traditional trio of paint, wallcovering, and mirror—it solves its space problems with floor-to-ceiling 18 x 18-inch polished granite panels. This highly reflective material has such a rich appearance that the room design needs only a handful of strongly styled pieces—one sofa, two chairs, one carpet, one coffee table, two urns, and one broken-pediment mirror—to complete it. Mustard-colored soffits a few inches in front of the walls conceal the lighting that seems to raise the white ceiling and, at the same time, push the walls farther away.

Windows

The most important question to ask before starting to design a window treatment is: What can this window contribute to this room?

From a space-planning perspective, a window with a good view can focus the eye on the outdoors and make the boundaries of the room seem farther away than they really are. Conversely, an ugly view will make you stop your gaze well short of the window, and the room will feel smaller than it is. Don't assume, however, that a view of a neighboring wall will automatically curtail your sense of spaciousness; if there is some element of interest—an ivy covering, for instance, or architectural detailing—the eye may be attracted outward. If you are on friendly terms with the owner of a wall that forms your view, you might ask if you can plant a fast-growing vine or install a lavabo on it.

Regardless of view, however, the mere existence of a window draws attention: it has a large, well-defined shape, it is different in texture and tone from the rest of the wall, and for a good part of the day it transmits at least some degree of light. Whether you want to exploit a view or hide it, a window is a ready-made focal point that lends itself to a wide variety of covering and framing treatments, all of which can help enhance the apparent size of a room.

A window treatment that blends in with the surrounding wall—white fabric with black dots against a white wall, for instance—will make the wall and window flow as one continuous space, while the pattern gently directs attention to the window. On the other hand, a treatment that contrasts with the surrounding wall—for instance, black fabric with white dots against a white wall—can rivet attention at the window with two possible effects: it can break up the flow of the wall and pull the window forward visually, making the room appear smaller; or, if the window and/or treatment occupy most of the wall, a riveting treatment can force the gaze out the window to space beyond the room. If you want to exploit the space-making qualities of light and airiness, but are not enchanted with your view, it might be safest to stick to window treatments that blend into the surrounding wall, but there can be exceptions: the design on page 170, for instance, uses a very bold treatment not to enhance any view but for its strong doubling effect in the adjacent mirrored wall.

Since a window treatment reaches away from eye level toward the ceiling, it can be a perfect vehicle for achieving the sense of large scale, bulk, and importance that you might be leery of trying anywhere else in a small room. In addition, the closer to the ceiling a window treatment is, the more it seems to defy gravity and helps to balance the inevitable bottom-heaviness of any room. In a room that has been pared down to hard edges in order to create both physical and illusory space, a voluminous window treatment can provide a compensating sense of softness and upholstery without taking up much real space.

Since windows are usually not in wear-and-tear locations, they are the perfect places to display fabrics, textures, and colors that you wouldn't dream of using on furniture or floors or even walls that are subject to more abuse. Draperies have the added advantage of usually being detachable and easily washed or dry cleaned.

The impact of a window treatment is not simply a matter of style but depends on how you blend three equally important elements: style, material, and color and pattern. For instance, a Roman shade in a stereotypical heavy fabric with a large bold stripe conveys a sense of seriousness and strength, but the very same style of shade takes on a lightness if the fabric is chintz, and an added softness if the pattern is a pale overall floral. Similarly, a venetian blind or a roller shade can send out any number of messages, depending on its color, trim, and pattern.

Window coverings come in all types of materials and styles and can be used alone or in combined layers. They can be mass-produced or custom made, or a combination that adds a custom dash to off-the-shelf products. You can, for instance, cover ordinary venetian-blind tapes with bright or patterned fabric to add an attention-getting vertical thrust to an otherwise horizontal treatment. You can have exquisitely delicate curtains made at great expense and hang them with confidence over store-bought pleated shades in a harmonizing color.

A window treatment can be fixed, operational, or a combination of both, like a stationary valance capping a roll-up solar shade, or even great swags of velvet permanently attached to a wall to form a frame for venetian blinds or pleated shades or an underlayer of retractable sheers. If you don't need all the elements of a window treatment to be retractable, permanently setting parts in place can save money on hardware and even on the amount of material needed to achieve the desired effect.

Materials

Fabrics

Fabrics can be hung in flat panels, gathered, pinch-pleated, draped and swagged, braided, twisted, or in-corporated into elaborate shade mechanisms (see the next section, "Window Treatment Components"). For loose gathers, figure on buying fabric twice the width of the window; for full gathers, budget for four times the width of the window.

Sheer fabrics can give a watery impression of the outdoor view and provide some glare control, but they don't protect your privacy at night.

Semi-sheer or meshlike fabrics provide a partial view while filtering out excessive light and maintaining privacy. If you are not sure how a fabric you like will perform, buy a yard, stretch it flat over a window for a few days, and test it in the following ways:

- Try reading a newspaper while facing the window, with the sun pouring in (winter is the best test time, since the sun is low on the horizon and seems to glare directly at eye level).
- As you go about your indoor business during the daytime hours, note if you like the view you see outdoors through the fabric.
- If the view is fine but there is more glare and less privacy than you like, pleating or gathering the fabric should resolve the problem.

Opaque fabrics block the view in and out, but, depending on their weight and color, may let in varying degrees of light and may allow your silhouette to be seen at night.

Linings can be used with opaque fabrics to produce darkness for bedrooms and home theaters, to create contrasting turnbacks, to protect a delicate fabric from the sun, to keep the color of the fabric from tinting the light in the room, and to help the treatment hang in a desired way (the weight of a bead chain sewn into the bottom hem can also influence how the treatment hangs).

Window-treatment fabrics are manufactured with the same pattern and color intensity on both sides. If the material you prefer to use is upholstery, sheeting, or dressmaking fabric, the underside may be paler, it may look like a reverse image of the front or like TV "snow," or it may be just a collection of long threads bearing no resemblance to the front at all. Unless you are absolutely sure that your window-treatment design will not reveal any of the underside, you may want to stick with standard window fabric or use linings.

Wood

Rigid materials such as match stick, bamboo, and woven wood slats are most commonly seen in manufactured shades that roll up from the bottom, but can also be used as inserts in shutters or shoji screens. These materials are good for protecting privacy and controlling glare, and can provide a reasonable impression of the outdoor view.

Solar Mesh

Solar mesh is a woven plastic that lets light pass through pin-dot holes. Window coverings made of this material provide an amazing degree of view yet almost total privacy at the same time. The tighter the weave, the less you will be able to see out; the closer you stand to this material, the more you can see, meaning that people across the street shouldn't be able to see in at all, even at night. This material, available in both roller shades (called solar shades or tech shades) and pleated shades, can also be used for custom Roman shades. It may be the benchmark for materials that simultaneously conceal and reveal.

Reflective Coatings

Reflective coatings that bounce heat and glare back to their source are often available on manufactured products, but can't be applied after manufacture. However, separate transparent reflective products in shade or curtain form are available to use as the element of the window treatment laid closest to the window. Transparent reflective films in bronze, cool and warm gray, and blue and green tones may also be applied directly to the window surface; the bronze and warm gray tones seem to be best for controlling heat without tinting the view. If you plan to install new windows, consider tinted glass.

These are the most common window-treatment materials but they don't by any means exhaust the possibilities—clear plastic tubes strung in rows, bed sheets, perforated metal, wood grille, fish net, and shawls are all perfectly valid options. You could, if you want, cover a valance with carpet, write poetry on the panels of a shoji screen, paint palm fronds on the window panes—again all perfectly valid and worth experimenting with.

Window-Treatment Components

All of these components can be used alone or as parts of multilayered window treatments. Most can be automated with small motors that can be easily hidden behind the window treatment, but because of the wiring involved, motorization has to be specified at the time an order is placed.

Drapes and Curtains

Drapes and curtains, which have become synonymous over the years, can be installed in three basic ways: 1) attached in a fixed position directly on the wall or to a furring strip attached to the wall; 2) on hooks attached to a mechanical track that takes pinch-pleated or soft S-pleated fabric; 3) on a pole that runs through rings or a pocket sewn into the back of the fabric (the rings can be plain or decorative hoops, loops of fabric, chain—whatever a pole can pass through). Poles may seem the simplest and most given to decorative flourishes, but moving the fabric back and forth on them is not always easy, and, depending on the thickness of the pole and the weight of the fabric, poles may have to be supported every few feet.

Roller Shades

Roller shades roll up to about four inches in thickness, depending on their length and material. They can be laminated with smooth, thin fabric or wallpaper of your choice, or hand-painted so long as the material is porous enough to absorb the paint rather than leaving it on the surface to crack as the shade curves and straightens during the rolling process. The bottom rail of a roller shade can be trimmed to coordinate or contrast with the surroundings. Laminated roller shades are invariably opaque; their only virtue in terms of view/glare/privacy is their ability to cover or uncover a window in seconds.

Special blackout shades, which provide maximum light control for places like bedrooms and video rooms, are not actually black and can be laminated or painted just like any other shade.

Solar shades use a roller-shade mechanism with a woven plastic material that lets light pass through pin-dot holes. They come in a variety of neutrals that will harmonize with almost any additional elements you may use in your window treatment.

Pleated Shades

Manufactured pleated shades pull up accordion-fashion and come in almost any material, including solar mesh, blackout, and reflective-coated materials, and any color, pattern, and degree of transparency; they produce a hazy view when made of semi-sheer fabric or solar mesh, and swiftly pull up to reveal a clear view. When down, they retain a pleated edge. Of all the window-covering mechanisms, pleated shades are probably the most compact when pulled out of the way.

Roman Shades

Roman shades pull up into large, soft pleats to reveal clear views, and lower into flat panels. They can be made of almost any material, with any thickness and any degree of see-through, but if they are semi-sheer or solar they will provide a hazy view and varying degrees of privacy when let down. They also can be knife-pleated, but must have an opaque lining to hide the pleating mechanism and will therefore not provide any view when lowered.

Austrian Shades

Austrian shades consist of fabric evenly gathered in a vertical line from top to bottom, creating an appearance of fullness even though they lie fairly flat against a window. When made of semi-sheer material, Austrian shades provide a hazy view and protect privacy when lowered. Very thick fabrics may not pull up very high and could, unless the stack is almost completely on the wall above the window, diminish the view even when open.

Balloon Shades

Balloon shades gather from the bottom as they pull up into billows, creating more three-dimensional volume than Austrians as they rise; they flatten from the top as they are lowered. Although they can be made of almost any thickness of fabric, if they are semi-sheer they will provide a hazy view and protect privacy when lowered.

Venetian Blinds

Venetian blinds pull up for a clear view, and tilt for partial view, privacy, and glare control. The wider the slat, the fewer are needed, and the more distance there is between the slats for looking out (dark slats, however, may produce a prison-bar effect) and the shorter the stack at the top when they are completely retracted. They are manufactured in wood, metal, and sometimes plastic; the metals come in the widest variety of colors. All venetians can be equipped with contrasting or trimmed tapes. Tilting the upper sides of the slats away from the room creates the best view and the greatest privacy, and keeps the dusty side of the slat almost invisible from the room side. When venetian blinds wider than four feet need to be washed, they have to be taken apart, and soaped and rinsed slat by slat. Narrower venetians usually can be dismounted, dunked up and down as a unit in a bathtub of sudsy water, rinsed with a hand-held shower attachment, and reinstalled at the window to dry.

Vertical Blinds

Verticals, which move from side to side, can be stacked on the wall, leaving the entire window surface free. They can be made of fabric or solar mesh, in addition to solid or perforated metal, plastic, or wood (which tends to be a bit clumsy in a vertical format). Like the horizontal venetians, they can retract or cover a window completely, while their slats can be tilted to adjust for view, glare, and privacy. They are not suitable coverings for windows that slide up and down, however (see the sidebar on page 168).

Shojis and Shutters

Shojis and shutters are window treatments that can employ almost any type of material suspended within solid structural frames. They can slide side to side or up and down on tracks, they can pivot in and out or up and down on hinges, or they can tilt in and out on a central swivel. The inserts can be glass, fabric, paper, grillwork, woven woods, alabaster—just about anything; shutter inserts also can be the same solid material as the frames, as well as fixed or movable louvers. Opened shojis and shutters don't always have to take up window room; they can be hinged to stack on a wall or slide into wall-mounted pockets.

Valances

Valances run across the tops of windows to create a finished look; without some kind of valance, most rooms look incomplete. Their value as space makers derives from their ability to make a window appear larger by drawing the eye beyond the frame; a tall valance mounted mainly on the wall above the window suggests that the window continues behind it. All valances should fall about four inches below the top of the window frame to smooth over the clutter of frame, wall line, and the mechanisms and stack of any other window treatment component or backlighting you may use. A valance on its own can be two or three inches from the wall; to create a pocket to hide the mechanism of a second treatment component, it should be about five inches off the wall. In calculating how deep a valance should be to hide other mechanisms, remember that at least one treatment component usually can be installed inside the window-frame recess. Valances can be made of almost anything: wood molding, upholstered board, wallpapered board, perforated metal, grillwork; they can also be formed of abbreviated sections of full treatments—a valance can be, for instance, a stationary version of a pulled-up Roman, Austrian, or balloon shade.

ENLARGING THE WINDOW

Physically enlarging a window is an expensive proposition, and in some cases—apartments, for instance—requires permission from landlords and next-to-impossible-to-get permits from local government agencies.

Clever use of window treatments, on the other hand, can give you a window as large as you want, at a fraction of the cost and with a lot less hassle. For instance:

- Installing the treatment directly on the ceiling, rather than at the top of the frame, can give the illusion that the window stretches all the way up to the ceiling. Letting the treatment extend past the sill and down to the floor can make the window appear to be longer than it really is. (If the sill is more than a few inches deep, however, the treatment would have to be hung a distance out from the window, which may make the room seem smaller.)
- Extending the treatment beyond the width of the window will make the window appear proportionately wider.
- Extending the treatment across a section of wall that separates windows can make it appear that you have one huge window rather than two small ones. (If the separator is a corner, however, covering it with window treatment may have the opposite effect; see page 176).
- Extending the treatment across the entire wall that contains the window can make it seem you have a wide wall made of nothing but light and air.
- When the treatment extends well beyond the frame, the illusion of a larger window can be reinforced by warm white or daylight fluorescents installed in a four-inch-deep space behind the top of the treatment; overlap the ends of the tubes to prevent dark spots.
- Reflective materials like mirrored or chrome strips applied to windowsills and the recesses of the window frame can make a window opening appear larger than it is.

BALANCING BULK

ABOVE: In a small room with big chubby seating, a large-scale window treatment in similar tones can carry the generous upholstered feeling up to the ceiling, keeping the room soft and comfortable while minimizing bulk. Both sheer and opaque layers fall to the floor to increase the sense of height. The large floral print echoes the scale of the furniture. Other space-expanding techniques include placing the few splashes of color—lamp shade, framed poster, dining chair upholstery—at the farthest reaches of the room and on roughly the same plane. The see-through coffee table with its arrangement of glass objects prevents the eye from focusing on the center of the space and pulling the walls in.

WHAT MECHANISM FOR WHAT WINDOW?

Window treatments that move up and down lose a great deal of their flexibility when installed over windows that open in a side-to-side motion. If the window is opened so much as a crack, the entire treatment must be retracted or suffer sun, rain, or pollution damage along the edge exposed to the elements; wind passing through the slimmest opening could noisily bang the entire window treatment around and perhaps dislodge it from its mountings. For the same reason, treatments that move side to side are a problem when installed for up-and-down windows. For this reason, always match the movement of your window treatment to the movement of your window.

A WALLFUL OF WINDOW TREATMENT

BELOW: This small studio has two average-size but off-center windows. Using the same fabric for both the wall and the flat, ungathered window treatment gives the impression that the entire wall is windowed, but the owner has opted deliberately to expose only two sections. The sheers stay flush to the window; letting them fall to the floor would have involved pushing them out another six to eight inches into the room in order to clear the radiator cover. The flat over-layer draws attention to the windows through the use of a bold exposed lining, peeled back on the diagonal to help slow the eye as it travels along the wall. Room-side recessed lighting fixtures aimed at the opened sections boost the sense of the windows as gateways to light and space. The room-length valance obscures the fact that the windows do not actually rise to the ceiling.

Other space-expanding techniques include a dark geometrical pattern painted on the armoire, which gives it the look of a window or French door; backlighting above the armoire and the floor lamp to its side; and a voluptuous oversize urn in the dining area, which implies that the room is big enough for such large gestures.

TENT STYLE

ABOVE: A flat, vertically striped window treatment at the far end of this living/dining room exaggerates the room's long, narrow shape, turning a liability into an asset. Whereas a solid color could have pulled the window forward, the bold stripes draw the eye along the entire length of the room and up the wall. The lining is flapped back tent style as if to reveal another room beyond the window-hugging vertical blinds; a solid bold color works in the flaps because they form an upward-moving diagonal. Taken to its maximum length, the space is then doubled in width by

a fully mirrored side wall. Because the window stripe is so prominent and stakes out such a broad, high expanse, the doubling effect is exceptionally strong. A built-in soffit above the painted wall continues the valance line and at the same time reinforces the ability of the soffit-less mirror wall to dissolve convincingly into a doubled space. The window treatment was created from inexpensive mid-weight printed cotton, with special attention paid to lining up the stripes from valance to hanging panel. The flaps are held open with a decorative hook on the wall and a threaded loop, or blind eye, sewn into the fabric.

ROOM WITHIN A ROOM

BELOW: A window treatment surrounds the bed in this small room to give the illusion of an extra-height four-poster, and the suggestion of a windowed room within a room. The upward sweep of pinch-pleated fabric at the four corners immediately draws the eye to the ceiling, where a ruffled valance anchors the treatment. A slightly paler soft piping finishes off the top of the valance and smooths the transition to the ceiling. The entire arrangement is attached to the ceiling with only the slenderest of poles to keep the corner panels in a straight vertical line. The ceiling directly over the bed is fabric covered to enhance the illusion of the bed as a tall room within a room. Using the bed as a focal point would seem to violate the principle of keeping atten-

tion away from the center in a small room, but the fabric's pale color and vertical movement keep the eye moving up and away.

The details of the bed treatment are carried to the window, but with some differences. Bold colored café curtains and valance draw the eye out to the farthest boundaries of the room, and polished fabric provides a touch of reflectivity. The café rod is six to eright inches from the window to permit room for a hand to reach in to adjust the controls of the hidden heating and cooling equipment. A support for the center of the café rod slips through the folds of the full-length back curtain. Both the bed and window treatments were created from elements ordered from consumer catalogs for windows.

FINDING THE COMPONENTS

For shades and manufactured or custom fabric treatments, check your phone book under windows or window treatments. Fabric and upholstery shops may also double as window-treatment fabricators. Shojis and shutters may be under window treatments or under lumber or cabinetry. In some regions, there may be a separate listing for shoji makers. Blinds are usually listed under venetian. For custom components, it is best to use local specialists, since large retailers will farm the work out to them anyway. For manufactured components, it is best to call around to the shops first in order to narrow down your research to the least number of sources; when you buy you may have to pay a measurement fee, which guarantees that the treatment will be replaced if it doesn't fit. It is also possible to achieve great savings by using discount mail-order sources for most or all components, but if you make a mistake in the measurements, you won't be able to return the goods for exchange or refund.

SIMPLE SOLUTION

FACING PAGE: A simple flow of richly pleated sheers smoothly disguises visual clutter in this tiny bedroom: radiator; air conditioner; a busy, confining view; the frames and sills of two windows; and the structural column that separates them. Focusing some artificial light toward the bottom of the gathers creates the illusion that the windows reach to the floor. The simple flow of curtains repeats in the bronze mirrors on the closet and the structural column on the opposite side of the room; bronze matches the low intensity of daylight filtered through the sheers.

Blackout shades installed behind the sheers insure nighttime privacy and undisturbed sleep at sunrise; the room side of the shades is a pale color to create a sense of daylight even when the shades are drawn. Low lamps with opaque shades keep the eye moving in a horizontal sweep at roughly windowsill level.

ACCENTUATING THE HORIZONTAL

ABOVE: The Oriental lines of this room easily accommodate a clean, horizontally framed view, but at certain times of the day and certain times of the year, the angle of the sun creates uncomfortable glare inside. To expose the view, Roman shades pull up into soft, flat pleats whose edges make the arrangement look like the borders of an architectural cornice. Fitted snugly to the ceiling to imply that the windows reach maximum height, these shades create a strong horizontal line reinforcing the flow from living room to dining area. A mirrored wall doubles the perceived space and further emphasizes the wide-open feeling.

When let down to block glare or create privacy, the Roman shades reveal a flat, calm expanse of fabric—no gathers, no pleats. The fabric's spare pattern of wood-toned strokes brings the furniture colors upward and bounces the eye away from the coffee table, a focal piece that would otherwise pull the rest of the room in toward the center.

FANCY FLOURISHES

BELOW: As if to prove conclusively that you can have any style you want without sacrificing a sense of spaciousness, this window treatment borrows the flourishes of a nineteenth-century ball gown but deploys them in flat panels that make no pretense at covering the expanse of glass. To create an illusion of width, identical panels also hang in front of adjacent wall sections. The impression of fullness comes from two sources: the draping of the fabric into loose knots, and the plain self-fabric ties, strung across the top molding, that simultaneously suggest both bows and gathers. The molding, which conceals the simple hardware supporting the fabric panels, is painted white rather than a matching ivory in order to help visually attach the window treatment to the ceiling. A one-piece radiator cover/bookcase, in a darker tone than the carpeting and the fabric panels, helps pull the radiator forward and make the window appear farther away. Very finely pleated shades provide glare control and privacy.

A lightweight cotton capable of holding a modified puff form is draped at the sides of the entrance to an adjoining home office; the fabric helps to separate the areas without the use of a more confining permanent divider. The side drapery was created by loosely stitching each puff to a flat band of fabric and attaching the band to wall hooks.

FAUX BALLOON SHADE

ABOVE: This casual arrangement of sheer fabric mimics the feeling of balloon shades while maintaining a flat profile that hugs the window. The balloon illusion balances the bulk of the sofa while the pale color draws the eye upward from it. Since the mirrored wall doubles the image, only one vertical panel is used (see reflection); the illusion created is that of one window flowing uninterrupted through two spaces. The feathery branches of the plant carry the eye gracefully across the structural column and into the mirror. The treatment required fabric roughly three times the length of the curtain pole, plus enough for the single vertical panel. (A do-it-yourselfer might want to set aside a week for occasional adjustments to get the drape of the fabric just right before inviting guests.)

RELYING ON VALANCES

FACING PAGE, TOP: Tailored balloon valances organize nonaligned, non-matching paned windows and a sliding door into a unified expanse of glass in this living/dining room. A mirrored wall doubles the line-up and creates the illusion of a large room almost surrounded by windows. The valance does not rise to ceiling height, since the resulting bulk would have overwhelmed the relatively small windows. Since privacy is not an issue on this fenced-in property, no additional window treatment was needed.

The valances draw attention up and away from the bulk of the centrally located four-seater ottoman (whose short legs give it a bit of a lift). The slim lines of the lamp table continue the windowpane pattern to the floor, while the potted tree smoothes over the structural differences between the window and the door.

CORNERING ATTENTION

BELOW: Simple gathered sheers stacked on the walls to either side of this windowed corner focus the eye on the view and make it possible to pull the chair deep into the corner. Positioning the curtain rings about 16 inches apart creates a deep, almost ruffled effect that draws the eye to the top of what is nothing more than a single length of fabric. The rod, cleanly mitered at the corner, is set high enough on the wall to let the fabric loop deeply without revealing the horizontal demarcation between window and upper wall. The fabric stops three inches below the windowsill; if it flowed down to the floor, the fabric would have called attention to itself rather than to the window.

White was chosen as an accent color to draw the eye through the pale yellow room and out the window. While eye-level colors normally should be the weakest because they tend to recede, bright art serves here to draw attention away from the bulk of the beds, while the white mats keep the eye on the path to the window.

UPHOLSTERY AT THE WINDOW

LEFT: Upholstered valances make these windows appear taller than they are; while the bottom roll hides the mechanism for the solar-mesh shade, the top two rolls cover nothing but wall. The shade is installed in the window-frame recess close to the glass. The valances' alternating colors carry the darker tones of the furniture toward the ceiling while the paler hue pulls the total arrangement back to the wall. Window placement in this room dictates the furniture arrangement: matching armchairs frame the single window while the long sofa (with pale upholstery to help it sink into the wall) accentuates the width of the double window. It is the bold window treatment, however, that grounds and centers the off-center windows.

BRAIDED ATTRACTION

LEFT: A child's room is also a part-time playground; it demands physical and psychological spaciousness and as much outdoor presence as possible. The same room, however, must be able to switch to maximum dimness in order to encourage sleep. Here, a tricolor braided swag draws attention up the wall, out the window, and away from an eye-catching novelty bed in the center of the room. The cobalt blue slats of the mini-blinds dissolve into a sky tone when opened and add to the dimness when closed. The braid softens the transition between the white wall and the block of blue created by the closed blinds; it repeats in the mirrors that dissolve the corner column into the wall. This soft braid required fabric half again as long as the finished length; a tighter braid could require up to two times as much fabric. Securing the end of the braid to the wall discourages children from trying to swing on it.

THE PARTIALLY CLAD WINDOW

FACING PAGE, TOP: The nighttime view from the wide expanse of window in this high-rise is dramatic and exciting, but during the day the world appears somewhat gray and unwelcoming. The peach and earth tone living/dining room seemed to huddle against, rather than expand into, the outdoors. Pleated shades halfway down solve the problem by revealing the balcony and outdoors but preventing the view from becoming an overwhelming focal point. The barely translucent fabric admits enough daylight to keep the windowed boundary light and airy; the pale peach tone keeps indoor light consistently sunny regardless of outdoor conditions. At night, the shades retreat in a flash—into a stack of neat knife pleats less than five inches deep—for maximum exposure of the view. The pleated shades are hung directly from the ceiling to create an illusion of height; their pale color helps draw the eye in one continuous sweep around the room. The warm peach-colored mirror covering the dining area wall doubles the expanse of window and pleated shade.

LESSONS FROM JAPAN

BELOW: Asian design themes combine clean lines and delicate filigrees to create a serene atmosphere that makes a room appear spacious even when it is not. In this small room shoji screens enhance the effect by suggesting a sequence of spaces continuing on the other side, as is customary in Japanese structures. In winter the shojis admit filtered light while blocking out rather claustrophobic views of a tiny, barren, fenced-in patio; in spring and summer the shojis slide sideways for a pleasant view of the patio, layered with growing things. The mirrored valance is light and airy while its smoke tone blends with the shoji frames; short extensions of the valance mirror into the top of adjoining beams add to the horizontal line. Warm white fluorescents tucked behind the shojis continue a sense of daylight into the evening hours. The rice paper and wood shojis were inexpensive off-the-shelf purchases.

PRIVACY VERSUS VIEWS

FACING PAGE: This windowed solarium receives a great deal of direct sunlight and has a stupendous wide-open view of sky and water. However, the room, often pressed into duty as a guest room, is vulnerable to the gazes of neighbors from the towers to the west and to morning glare from the east. The glare can be especially brutal during the coldest months, when the sun hangs low in the sky and its light is directly at eye level.

Solar shades, which provide total privacy and glare control while still permitting an impressionistic image of the outdoors, were the solution. The shades were chosen in the lightest color available in order to make them recede the farthest from the viewer and appear to attach themselves to the view rather than to the room. A four-inch wood valance, stained two tones lighter than the upholstery, helps sweep the eye up to the top of the window. The ceiling, however, contains a hint of color that pulls it down and makes the white shades appear farther away. A structural column has been mirrored to extend the open sense of window. Since for many people a view of this character takes on the quality of art, the window treatment is on the hard-edged side in order to perform as a frame. The short, hedgelike plants on the windowsill may block a bit of the view, but they also provide softness and a transition between indoors and outdoors.

The shoji screens turn the solarium into a private room for guests, but still transmit enough daylight to appear to be a large window when viewed from the adjoining room.

Built-ins

Planning for built-ins is more complex than buying freestanding furniture and dropping it into place, but there are many rewards: cleaner lines, the elimination of every inch of wasted space, and, perhaps the best bonus of all, an exact fit that can give you the opportunity to use more substantial freestanding pieces than you thought you had room for. Built-ins add an architectural quality and can change the proportions of a room—for instance, installing a wall-to-wall, floor-to-ceiling unit at the end of a narrow room will make it appear wider. Because much planning goes into them, built-ins tend to become focal points.

Ready-mades tend to come in widths divisible by 12, but built-ins come in the sizes you actually need—a bookcase for that 73-inch wall, for instance, a desk for that 27½-inch-deep niche, or a 25-inch-deep credenza that will eliminate the need for a seam in your wall-to-wall carpet. Built-ins are also made with extra edging that can be whittled to accommodate off-kilter walls, ceilings, and floors.

Even when the measurements of your home and readily available units are a perfect match, built-ins have the added virtue of being able to go around corners, describe curves, and swing back to create formal enclosures without using walls. Since you call the shots, you can have whatever you want. One of the greatest advantages of a built-in is that the arrangement looks deliberate rather than arbitrary or desperate.

Among the possibilities for built-in treatment are bookcases, armoires, beds, entertainment centers, lighting coves, desks, bars, consoles, islands, dining banquettes, sofas, platforms, chairs, dividers, and any object that can be wall mounted or raised above floor level to allow space to flow freely underneath.

Built-in storage makes it possible to use strangely sized doors and drawers from other eras or other countries, or indulge in moldings, materials, or finishes that no manufacturer seems to be using. It lets you take full advantage of the empty spaces between the studs in your walls. A built-in that straddles a room boundary can serve both rooms; some drawers or shelves can open into one room, while some open into the other. A TV on a deep open shelf of a room divider can be swiveled to serve whatever room the household happens to be gathered in. Drawers can be inserted into the side of a staircase or, with recessed handles, into the risers.

A staircase can also become a bookcase, with the volumes inserted into the risers. To protect the spines of the books, push them back at least two inches into the risers. (Even if you don't care whether the book spines get scuffed, don't let the books extend out onto the treads; any reduction of the foot space on the treads can cause fatigue and accidents. For the same reasons, don't plan on building a staircase to hold books taller than 7½ inches.)

Built-in seating allows for storage underneath—

skis under a sofa, for instance, even power tools inside a dining area banquette. With enough built-in seating storage you might be able to eliminate the need for one of your closets altogether and incorporate its footage into a room. Built-in tables let you dine in foyers or hallways while still permitting people to walk around you. And, of course, a built-in ironing board is a great convenience—push it up against a wall when you're finished, close a door over it, and walk away.

While built-ins cost more than ready-mades, they are not that much more expensive than buying ready-mades and then trying to cut them to fit. Incorporating wiring into built-ins is easy; even the most expensive ready-mades leave wires dangling all over. And if you have a ready-made you love, a cabinetry shop can incorporate it into a built-in. Make sure to study the Appendix, "Professionals and Trades," to learn how to work with the relevant trades and specialties.

WORKING WITH THE PERSON WHO IS GOING TO MAKE AND INSTALL YOUR BUILT-IN

- Study the construction of the room. What will the built-in be attached to? Concrete? Masonry? Plaster lathe? Drywall over studs? Ask how the fabricator—the person who is going to build and install the unit—intends to attach the unit.
- Be as specific as possible in words and measured drawings and examples of hardware. Get the fabricator to put in writing the hardware and material order numbers, installation methods, and estimates of final cost and delivery dates.
- A full-height unit can fool the eye into perceiving that a room is *smaller* than it actually is. Allow some space above and below the unit to make it clear that the room does not end where the unit begins. Consider installing light strips in the voids.
- Built-ins that go all the way down to the floor are generally installed after tile, stone, or wood, but before carpeting; wall-mounted items should be installed after carpeting. You may be able to negotiate to take your built-ins with you if you move, but since they are designed for a specific home, they may be worth more to the new household.
- Ask the fabricator about construction methods, including the location of laminate seams; the fabricator may be able to move the seams at a little extra expense or suggest a laminate line that runs wider.
- Plywood core material is the longest lasting for any kind of built-in construction.
- Polyester lacquer is more durable than standard lacquer and less costly to apply.
- Ask to see and test samples of hardware (plastic is a sign of cheap hardware and perhaps of a poor-quality fabricator). Check the bulk of hinges, especially if you are using glass doors; look at sample interior finishes for anything that will snag fabric or not wipe clean. Be wary of fabricators who say, "Don't worry, we'll take care of it"; find out exactly how they plan to take care of a problem.
- For upholstered built-ins make sure the cabinetry shop provides templates to the upholsterer. Consider a foam core wrapped in quilted material for a softer look. To avoid the cost of having to design and build a sofa from scratch, scout the stores and showrooms to find the style you want, check out seat comfort, including fillings, height and angle, and ease of rising, then have the manufacturer make one to the dimensions you need. In the end, it is cheaper to build cabinetry to dovetail with a sofa than to build a sofa to dovetail with cabinetry.
- The best time to order is right after major holidays; fabricators tend to be swamped just before holidays, and the quality of the work will probably not be as high as it could be. You also may have to pay a premium to get your job expedited.
- Learn as early as possible the schedules of the tradespeople and manufacturers you will be dealing with. For instance, many specialty shops close down for August; upholstery fabric manufacturers traditionally close down in July. The fabricator you choose may traditionally leave town for a week or two after New Year's or be planning a maternity leave. Ask.

BUILT-IN CHANGES THE FLOOR PLAN

BELOW: A long, curved, built-in sofa rescued a strange layout that put what looked like a dining alcove at a far remove from the kitchen. The alcove wasn't big enough for traditional furniture, but the built-in 12-foot seating unit works beautifully, hugging the window wall and turning the corner to include half of the new dining area as a living room extension. A shelf built into the sofa back serves as a radiator/air conditioner cover under the larger window and continues as a narrow sofa table for the balance of the unit. The entire structure is 32 inches deep and made of plastic-laminated wood and foam padding. The recessed base makes rising easier and also lets the floor extend as far as possible; the recess can be three to six inches high and no more than one third of the depth of the seating area. Mirroring the wall above the sofa increases the apparent size of the space. Bordered carpet tiles direct the gaze to travel the length and breadth of the space below eye level—and through the glass-topped open-frame coffee tables.

FACING PAGE, BOTTOM: A glass block window on the wall opposite the largest real window opens out the narrowest part of the room, while surrounding mirrors double the results. An open custom-made storage box 12 inches deep runs across the back wall well below eye level, emphasizing width and providing open storage for magazines, art books, old LPs and a turntable, and a compact contemporary audio system; wall mounting lifts the bottom up a few inches to let the floor flow through. To further distract from narrowness in this area, shallow striped soffits containing egg-crate baffled downlights draw the eye upward; a slightly darker ceiling color is carried a few inches down into the soffit to enlarge the ceiling. The two side chairs are spare enough to take up little space, but their bold forms give them the same presence as larger upholstered pieces.

TOP, RIGHT: In the living room extension a cabinet built in flush to the wall contains the TV, a dry bar, and storage for the adjacent dining area; the cabinet is raised several inches above the floor to let the lower wall appear to be an extension of the floor.

A BANQUETTE FOR A TIGHT SPOT

ABOVE: In a foyer that was too small for a dining suite, a built-in banquette creates a comfortable dining area and still leaves a generous passage to the living room beyond. A screen of brass rails, attached to the ceiling and seating with brass collars, serves to formally define the dining area without cutting off visual flow.

Even if the foyer had been large enough for a standard table and chairs, they would have looked as though the owners had placed them there not by choice but because no other spot was available. The banquette and screen of brass rails, however, convey the sense that the owners achieved exactly what they desired.

NONSTOP SOFA

ABOVE: Built-ins helped change this tiny area into a living/dining room that seats up to twelve and yet maintains the airiness of an art gallery. The seat of the wraparound sofa is 18 inches high, the same height as the seats of the freestanding dining chairs that are pulled up to the table at mealtime. The sofa is 30 inches deep (freestanding sofas are usually 36 inches deep), which makes the unit deep enough for living room relaxation but, with the use of back pillows, shallow enough to permit diners to sit upright at the table.

The unbroken line of the sofa as it wraps around the kitchen pass-through and clings almost all the way along the longest wall increases the apparent length of the room and draws the eye to the open spaces outside the window. The ficus tree, with most of its delicate foliage massed above eye level, softens the hard-edged urban view and keeps the view from appearing like just another confining wall. To avoid breaking the long view, a ceiling-mounted adjustable spot was used in lieu of a chandelier or pendant. Mirroring the wall above the sofa unit doubles the size of the area. The mirror's vertical lines draw attention upward while the chrome moldings along the other two sides of the room create an ambiguous reflective ceiling-wall boundary.

The sideboard at left was custom built just deep enough to hold its largest object, a 13-inch-screen TV on a pull-out swivel device. Uplight sconces at either end anchor the sideboard and ensure that its placement does not appear arbitrary. There was no need for a built-in radiator cover—the original was simply painted the same recessive white as the walls.

A SIMPLE SHELF CREATES AN ALCOVE

ABOVE: Built-ins don't have to be large or eye-catching. In this school-child's room the shelf over the bed contains downlights for ambient illumination, and combines with the freestanding bookshelves at right to suggest an alcove for the bed. The top of the light unit can be used for storage or display; a stenciled border circles the room at the same level, drawing the eye upward.

The top of the dresser curves out to become a desk and reaches all the way to the bed to serve as a night table. The shelves and dresser/desk are covered in a plastic laminate that mimics bleached wood; both the surfaces and the bedspread are a shade lighter than the walls so that the eye is drawn to objects rather than boundaries (a bedspread lighter than its surroundings also tends to look cleaner than it actually is).

MAXIMUM STORAGE AND FLOOR AREA

BELOW: A built-in dining unit maximizes both storage and floor area in this room. The table and buffet top form one right-angled wall-hugging unit in tones that match the wall; the arrangement seems to enlarge both the dining area and the living room simultaneously. The overhead china cabinet rises all the way to the ceiling and angles back on the diagonal into a shallow, open-ended bookcase over the buffet. The sofa is not built in, but is a sectional custom-built to fit the space. Since the central section is a pull-out bed, the coffee tables are small and light to make them easy to move away.

TRANSPARENT DIVIDER

ABOVE: This small studio gained a separate bedroom and dining area when a curved glass block wall was erected to enclose the banquette. The circular neon ceiling fixture sets up the dining room boundaries without taking up physical or visual space. To the right of the curved wall, a fluorescent strip illuminates the step to the raised bedroom; to the left is a long built-in that switches from a desk in the living room to a dresser in the bedroom. The box spring is set into the raised floor, with only enough of the mattress exposed to allow easy bedmaking. Wiring for the lamps also runs under the raised floor. The headboard is the back of the dresser, which, with a 30-inch-wide passage to the closet, forms a dressing area. Behind its sliding doors, the closet contains shelves in the center and long sections for hanging garments on each side; a mirrored back wall and a compact fluorescent that backlights the door cutouts suggest additional space beyond.

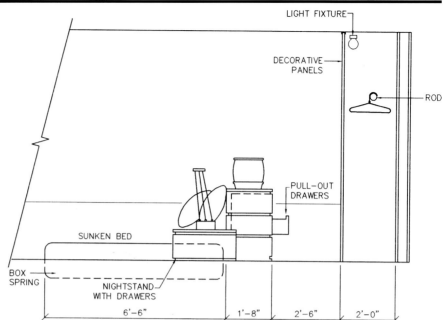

Sleeping Area

OUTWITTING STRUCTURAL ELEMENTS

ABOVE: Built-ins may have been the only way to make maximum use of this strangely shaped space. To minimize the division the large supporting wall creates in the living room area, a raised unifying floor runs diagonally in front of it two steps up from the base floor. This platform becomes the staging area for a complex arrangement of furnishings; their varying heights sweep the gaze around the room and away from the offending wall. The eye moves from the highest element, the built-in sofa, to a matching ottoman that straddles the living room/dining area boundary, then across the steps to a small wedge of platform on the other side of the wall that doubles as a seat at a small table that stands on the original floor. Mirroring and windows add spaciousness at the perimeters, while a piece of sculpture keeps any attention in the middle of the area rooted toward the bottom and the flow of the steps.

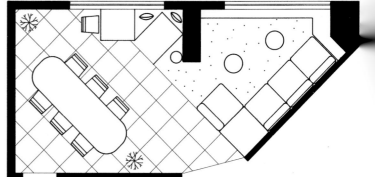

BUILT IN TO SAVE MONEY

BELOW: In a room of otherwise completely freestanding furniture, there is one major built-in: the mirror. For about half the price of a framed mirror of the same size, a large piece of mirror was attached directly to the wall with the special adhesive tar used for mirrored surfaces, and framing strips were attached directly to the wall around it. Since the mirror is completely supported by the wall, no special structural work was needed for the frame. The frame blends with the other tones in the room to avoid calling attention to itself and distracting from the space-expanding properties of the mirror. The client had fallen in love with a dark, intricately patterned fabric that would have grabbed too much attention as a king-size bedspread—and drawn the walls in too—so strips of the fabric were used instead to create a path through a cool, pale background to the mirror.

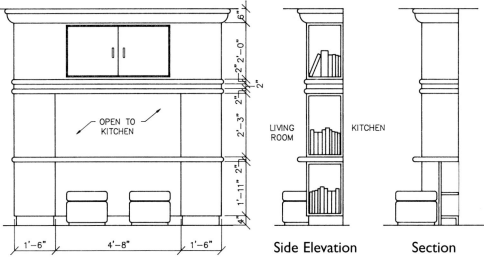

OPEN TO KITCHEN

1'-6" 4'-8" 1'-6"

6"
2'-2" 2'-0"
2"
2"
2'-3"
2"
1'-11" 2"
4"

LIVING ROOM   KITCHEN

Side Elevation   Section

Kitchen/Living Room

DIVIDE AND CONQUER

FACING PAGE: The advertisements for this apartment referred to a kitchen next to a living/dining room, but everyone who looked at the space knew it just wasn't big enough for all those functions. However, cutting a pass-through into the kitchen wall and extending the counter into a dining surface made the advertising claims come true. Kitchen storage, partly accessible from the living room, is above the pass-through and on both sides, which were fitted with bookcases facing the passages at either end. Emphatic wood molding emphasizes the breadth of the unit and gives it enough of an architectural presence to balance the massive obelisk on the other side of the room. Small uplights on the windowsills are used at night to compensate for the loss of space-enhancing natural light.

UNOBTRUSIVE ROOM DIVIDER

ABOVE: To create formal definition for the dining area without cutting off the view of the large classical window, a buffet structure is hung on two substantial columns and used as a room divider. The midsection of the buffet contains storage accessible to the dining area, while the curved end sections open on hinges toward the living room; the columns open toward the living room for display, and do not continue all the way through the buffet, which is supported only by the bottom sections. A cabinet shop sprayed a stone finish onto the columns.

A faux representation of architectural detail and climbing plants on the arched window makes the window appear even larger and gives the impression that the living room area is in the wide outdoors; drapery would have shrunk the window.

A POORLY PLACED BATHROOM DOOR

BELOW: Standard store-bought pieces might have fit into this space, except for two problems: the owners had two leather-covered chaises they loved and wanted to use, and a traditional furniture arrangement would have left some seats squarely facing the bathroom door. Moving the bathroom door into the foyer would have been very costly; moving the door into the walk-in closet would have resulted in a loss of storage space.

A built-in, three-step platform created storage and seating on the wall opposite the bathroom, let the two chaises constitute the only furniture in the living room area, and created strong diagonals that draw the eye along the longest lines in the space. In the arrangement the chaises face away from the bathroom; although the platform forms a wedge pointing in that direction, nobody sits on a point—the wide edges of the platform seating also face away from the bathroom.

Recessing the steps creates the sense of space flowing under the platform; each riser is equipped with a fluorescent strip. The platform in the far corner constitutes storage for out-of-season clothes and bedding. A third, lower platform section at the end of the tan chaise serves as a lamp table and an end table for the ottoman.

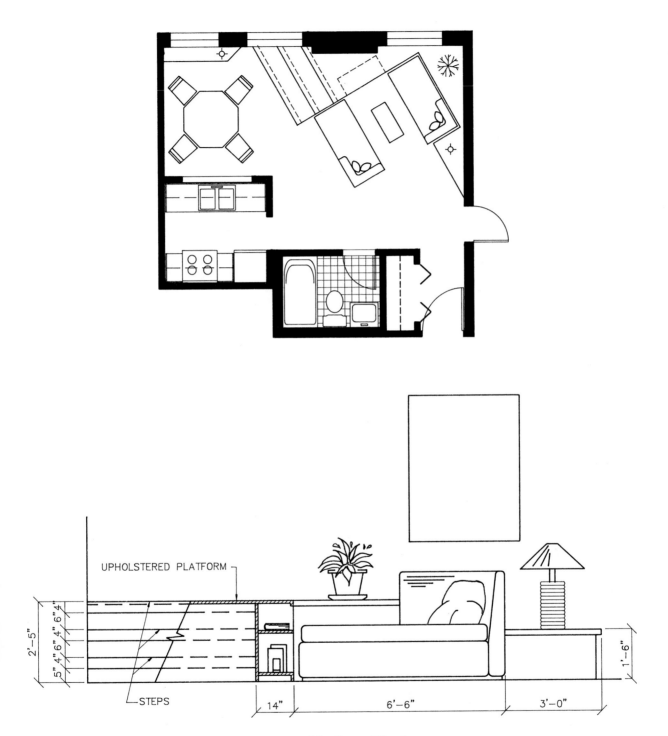

UPHOLSTERED PLATFORM

STEPS

2'-5"

5" 4" 6" 4" 6" 4"

14"

6'-6"

3'-0"

1'-6"

**Section of 3–Step Platform
with Storage and Chaise Longue**

MAKING ROOM FOR LARGER PIECES

ABOVE: This tiny den was able to accept a bold, chunky love seat after everything else in the room was installed flush to the walls. The shelved units were store bought, with the recessed lighting unit built in snugly above them to give an overall custom look; leaving the space above the downlights open lets the ceiling float like a canopy. The only other built-in is the desk that bridges two shelved units and extends into the room only far enough to hold a computer and keyboard; the corners are beveled to keep them from obstructing access to the love seat or the opposite storage unit. The footstool doubles as a seat at the computer. The mirrored wall over the love seat suggests additional space beyond.

RECONFIGURING THE BOX

ABOVE: Custom built-ins made it possible to break up the boxy quality of this small bedroom, install maximum storage, and still retain a sense of generous floor space and smooth passages. The long lines of the unit at left curve out from the dressing table into a standard-depth dresser and then into slim-doored storage with room for a TV on a pull-out pop-up mechanism. The far end of the unit disappears entirely to reveal a large chair-and-a-half curved around the bottom of a structural pillar. The base of the chair pulls out for easy retrieval of stored sports equipment. A steady de-crease in the width of the dresser unit made it possible to install the bed at an angle without blocking the walkway. The correspondingly angled built-in headboard contains wedge-shaped shelves directly above the bed and, to the side, a rounded unit that at the touch of a latch glides away on casters to reveal an attached bin with more than enough room to store a duvet. The depth of the space hides a locked compartment for precious jewelry. All the finishes are lacquer. Over the bed, a dropped soffit creates a canopy that echoes the lines of the headboard and contains downlights predirected for ambient as well reading light.

A DIVIDER CARVES OUT A NEW ROOM

ABOVE AND FACING PAGE: A custom room divider with a high opening turns one end of this small studio into a bedroom without cutting into the sense of free-flowing space. A raised platform defines the bed and dresser while allowing the living room floor to continue as far as possible around the divider; the dresser echoes the divider's shape. A built-in under the window covers the radiator and provides bookcases at either end. Mirroring makes the pillars and far wall seem to disappear. The bedroom also serves as a second conversation area during parties and as a playroom for visiting children.

The bedroom platform extends behind the far end of the divider and joins the wall-hugging curves of the sectional sofa to reinforce the continuous flow of space between the two areas as well as to create additional seating. This side of the divider contains a drop-down desk and hidden storage. The tall rounded near section opens to reveal an ironing board hung on the divider; a canister vacuum is housed in a pocket at the bottom of the curve, with hoses and brushes clamped above it. A recessed downlight is built in above the divider opening.

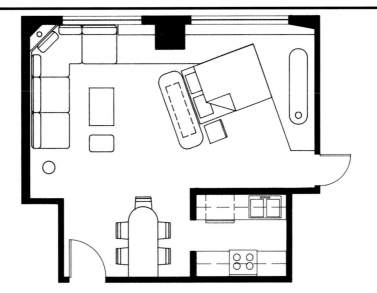

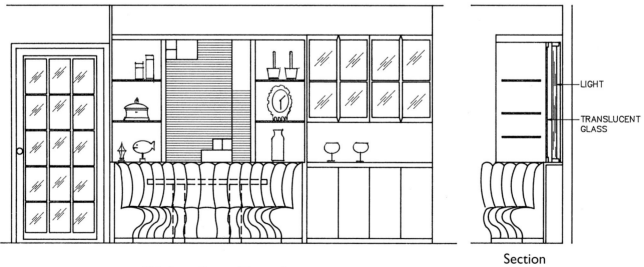

LIGHT

TRANSLUCENT GLASS

Dining–Area Elevation

Section

ANGLING FOR SPACE

FACING PAGE: Boldly colored built-ins gather this dining area into a space of its own without the use of any physical dividers to separate it from the living room. The upholstered banquette, seating up to four, is tucked into a blue-stained wall unit. Triangular glass shelves rise on either side of the back panel. The back-lit frosted panes in the cabinet at right echo the panes in the nursery door at left. Mirroring the space over the counter makes it resemble a pass-through. The corners of the rectangular granite tabletop have been sliced off to reduce mass and create generous passage.

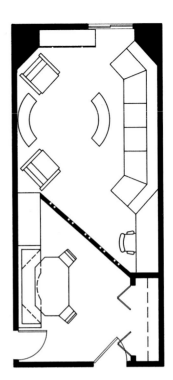

BELOW: The vivid blue color of the built-in in the dining area is repeated as an accent in the downlight cove over the sectional sofa. Since the end of the dining area is defined by 45-degree angles, the sofa ends with 45-degree sections that suggest a separately enclosed living room, again without the use of constraining walls. To create the impression that the sofa is built in, the desk was custom made to fit exactly at the end. A diagonally patterned floor directs traffic past the dining area and into the living room; the patterned stripe is an additional demarcation between the two functional areas.

Appendix: Professionals and Trades

Depending on how complex your space-expanding plans are, you may find you need the services of one or more of the following professionals and trades.

In some instances, the law may not let you do some jobs yourself. If you plan to move load-bearing walls or walls that contain electrical wiring or plumbing, you will need plans stamped by a registered architect (or engineer). The actual electrical, plumbing, and gas work may require government permits obtainable only by licensed workers.

In other instances, you may just need the advice of someone who has spent every working day developing and honing design skills. As always, you will get the best answers when you have the clearest questions, so try to hold off contacting anyone until you have done as much preplanning on your own as you can. Specialized services may be necessary at two distinct phases of the project, final planning and getting the actual work done.

Working with Design Professionals on a Final Plan

The term *design professional* traditionally covers architects, interior architects, and interior designers and decorators. If all you need is their advice, you should be able to arrange a consultation for an hourly fee. If you need them to create a design, you will be quoted a flat fee. Find out if the fee covers working drawings, estimating labor and materials, obtaining permits, and supervising the labor that will carry out the design. To some practitioners, supervision means visiting the site daily, while to others it means checking out and signing off on the completed job.

Shop not only for credentials but also for areas of expertise. Before making any appointments, spend some time on the phone making sure the person specializes in what you need—the titles of these professionals and the skills they may be required to have by law don't necessarily equip them to deal with your particular needs. For instance, while architects may have the most prestige of all the design professionals, are the most likely to be certified, and should have no trouble coming up with the perfect placements for your walls, they may not have much experience in creating the illusion of additional space, any special talent with color combinations, or the ability to suggest where to find the slimmest appliances.

Get recommendations from neighbors and friends who have had similar work done. Don't bother with design professionals who specialize in styles that don't attract you. Never, ever try to talk to any of them until you are ready to explain in words and maybe pictures exactly what you want. Be prepared to listen carefully and take notes when they start to share their ideas with you. If you don't understand something, ask.

TIMING IS ALL

Don't start any construction job unless you know that it can be finished, that you have enough money, and that the trades and fabricators involved can give you uninterrupted attention (for rare exceptions, see page 209). You can avoid premium fees and get better attention by scheduling your work when design professionals and trades are less likely to be busy—after, rather than before, major holidays, for instance.

To make out your own schedule of activities, find out if there are any times when your trades and fabricators are not likely to be available—some may traditionally close down at certain times of the year, or they may know that the materials you need are in short supply at other times. Then figure out which element of the entire job will take the longest to accomplish (usually something custom like built-ins, or murals, or mosaic tile), add in the time it will take to accomplish every job that has to be done before the

longest can even begin, plus the time it will take to finish all the subsequent jobs, and you have a good idea of how long the entire job will take from start to finish—assuming all the trades and fabricators will be available when you need them.

For instance, if your job is limited to painting, carpeting, and a custom floor-mounted dresser, figure the time it will take to build the unit, add the painting time at the beginning and the carpeting time at the end, and that is how long the job will take.

Mentally add on 10 percent of the days you've scheduled for the job as a cushion in case of unexpected events, and an additional week if the job is to take place in the summer or around year-end holidays, the most popular time for renovations. This way, any scheduling surprises should be pleasant ones. Whatever you do, do not issue party invitations until the entire job is completed to your satisfaction, right down to the furniture.

After years of grueling training and apprenticeship, *registered architects* take a long test that entitles them to the stamp that governments require for the filing of building plans. Some, but by no means all, registered architects use the letters RA after their names; you may have to ask. The designation AIA (American Institute of Architects) indicates membership in a professional organization and is not required in order to practice. Of all the design professionals, architects tend to be the most knowledgeable about local codes, regulations and permitting requirements, and the time needed to deal with them. In large cities, architects may charge an extra fee to cover the services of expediters who can speed paperwork through the bureaucracies.

A category of architects called *interior architects* focuses only on interior structures. They may—or may not—have experience specifying objects and finishes within those structures to best effect.

Some *interior designers* can do the working drawings for walls, electricity, and plumbing while others can't or won't. An interior designer can get an architect to review and stamp plans for a small fee to

cover the time involved. (This is not cheating; many "name" architects are themselves not registered but have people on their staffs who review and stamp for them.) Some interior designers specialize in office design or health care or hotels, areas where their expertise won't help you at all.

Decorators tend to limit themselves to colors, styles, finishes, and furniture arrangements, and produce sketches to indicate general effects but not working drawings. However, this may be exactly what you need and you may find someone who is far better at it than any of the more prestigious professionals could be.

Lighting consultants are the most knowledgeable about the effects of different lighting systems on materials, finishes, skin tones, and the sense of space. They also know how to save electricity without sacrificing effect. To get the best from a lighting consultant, he or she should be in on the final planning as early as possible, and perhaps working hand in hand with the other design professionals.

Kitchen designers specialize only in kitchens. The initials CKD (Certified Kitchen Designer) after their names indicate they have been tested and certified by the National Kitchen and Bath Association.

Stereo and security consultants may do working drawings for the wall framing to hold their installations, or simply provide data for drawings by architects, designers, or general contractors. Independent consultants can advise on all the manufactured lines that are available and on custom possibilities as well; they may charge for advice if you are not hiring them to carry out the job. Consultants attached to manufacturing firms tend to give advice quite freely, but their recommendations usually cover only those products their firms manufacture; if you already plan to stick to one manufacturer, using staff consultants will probably result in a lower bill for materials.

Landscape architects can help in the choice of indoor plants and give advice about growth rates, survival rates, pot sizes, built-in watering possibilities, and lighting and ventilation needs.

Working with Skilled Tradespeople to Get the Job Done

Before hiring tradespeople and fabricators, get recommendations from neighbors and friends (taking their tolerance levels and ability to be clear and work well with others into account) and make sure you see the jobs they've had done. Letters of recommendation from strangers don't mean much unless you get to see the actual work.

You can ask advice of tradespeople and fabricators—sometimes for an hourly fee, sometimes for free—without hiring them to do the actual job. If you hire them, you may find them giving you advice you haven't asked for. Listen carefully, since they have done this type of job many times before while you—no matter how much you have learned from your planning experience—are still a novice. In the end, however, you don't have to do it their way; they have to do it yours.

When you set out to actually hire someone, have ready a list of all the questions you need answered and get at least three ballpark estimates. Choose from the middle range. Preliminary estimates are usually, but not always, free. Ask for local references, ask to see one or more completed jobs, ask former clients if the work was completed on time and within budget.

PAYMENT AND TIPPING

With a few exceptions, the standard payment schedule is 25 percent upon signing the contract, two more 25-percent payments as long as the job is progressing according to schedule, and the balance when it is completed to your satisfaction. To give you time to check out the job, your contract can specify that the last payment is not due until a few days after completion; it also may specify that you can deduct a certain amount for each day the job is late, but try to be sympathetic to unforeseen problems like finishes not drying because the weather suddenly turns humid. Insist that you be notified as soon as possible of delays so you won't lose time at work—after all, the people you hire have the same access to weather forecasts that you do.

Fabricators of freestanding furniture will want payment in full in advance or upon delivery, but don't pay for built-ins until they are installed to your satisfaction. Avoid shops that refuse to take their own measurements, refuse to install, or insist on the balance before installation. If problems crop up after installation, a diplomatic approach is best, acknowledging probable error on both sides; this approach usually leads to a small negotiated fee to correct the problem. A hard-line "It's your fault" approach with fabricators will usually be frustrating and futile. Unless obvious fraud is involved, diplomatic negotiation is always better than complaining to government agencies or going to court.

Do tip delivery people, especially those who unwrap and take the packing materials away with them. A good rule of thumb is $2 per person for those who deliver and handle the packing material; $10 per person if they move the furniture into place for you. Be extra-generous if they accommodate to your schedule by delivering before or after working hours. Tip the people who install window treatments and mirrors. Tip electricians or other skilled trades when your home presents them with unforeseeable and difficult problems, or when they do special favors beyond the scope of the job description. Offer everyone iced drinks on hot days, coffee if they are working late.

AVOID MEASUREMENT PROBLEMS

If a fabricator or installer takes the measurements, he or she is responsible for correcting any errors. If you take the measurements, you are stuck with the problem. Make sure they write all the measurements down for you, but don't alienate them by acting as though you don't trust them—just say you're afraid you'll forget. Taking measurements also gives specialists a chance to visit the site and gauge the size of your elevator and the size and placement of your doors in order to prepare for any delivery problems.

Check licensing agencies, consumer agencies, and your local Better Business Bureau to see if there have been any complaints. Consider the personality of anyone you consider hiring—the ability to work well with a person may be worth a higher fee, but never sacrifice quality for the sake of compatibility.

Final estimates should be in writing and list specific tasks, materials order numbers and costs, work schedules, total costs, and payment schedules. Even if you plan to do some of the work yourself, get bids on all the tasks anyway in case it turns out that you don't have the time. Letting contractors or trades extend you credit may mean letting them take a lien on your property, a very risky venture.

For the greatest efficiency and least headaches, the work should occur in the order given below. Even if your particular job requires only two or three of these steps, the right sequence is still crucial.

1. *General contractors* organize all the trades on a job to make sure that a diversity of tasks gets carried out in the right order with the least amount of delay. They hire all the special trades, order the materials, schedule deliveries to coincide with the actual work and arrange to have debris removed. They take a percentage of the total cost as their fee, and may require you to pay for materials in advance. You can, of course, contract the various tasks yourself, but on a large job this can become quite a juggling act.

Make sure any contract you sign with a general contractor contains details about workmen's compensation and general liability insurance, licenses of subcontractors, work schedules, binding estimates, payment schedules, brands, order numbers, and quantities and prices of materials.

Responsible tradespeople and fabricators will be happy to let your lawyer review their contracts, but be very wary of any who insist their contracts are "just a formality" or push hard for immediate signatures. If you already have a lawyer, he or she may look at the contact for free; otherwise, you probably will have to pay an hourly fee. If there are problems, the solution should call for negotiation rather than major confrontation.

Lawyers love to tell horror stories, and yours may regale you with tales about other people's renovation disasters. Listen for the sake of clues that might help you avoid problems, but bear in mind that lawyers seldom hear about the happy renovation jobs. An architect or a contractor may be a better source than a lawyer for information on building codes.

Specialty subcontractors should submit shop drawings to you and your designer or architect so you can review exactly how the job will come together.

2. *The wall trades* handle demolition and construction of interior walls. Since demolition crews charge less than construction workers, it might make sense to divide a house-wide job between the two, but for a smaller job you may as well pay the construction people to do both parts.

The *plumber* should come in just before the demolition crew to remove fixtures and cap the water and/or gas outlets.

Electricians and plumbers move the wiring and pipes after demolition but before the construction of new walls. The wall trades are used to coordinating closely with them in this stage. This is also when any in-wall framing for speakers or security systems is built in. If you will need the electricians and plumbers to come back later in the job to install fixtures (see stage 7, below), make sure both parts of the job are included in the cost estimates.

3. *Painters* should now plaster and prime the new walls and give the ceiling its final coat, but the actual wall treatment should be held off until all the other dirty work is completed. If you are just smoothing out existing walls, your painters should be able to handle

minor plastering jobs, but if your walls are a total disaster, with deep holes and huge bulges, hire a plasterer.

4. *Floor installers* can now install most materials—stone, wood, vinyl, and ceramic tile. Outside of one exception, for built-ins that are raised above the floor, where they can get nicked or scratched during the carpeting process, all carpeting should be held off as long as possible. In fact, when a built-in goes all the way to the floor, there are two good reasons for installing carpeting last and around rather than under it: most built-ins tend to outlast most carpeting, and it's easier to level a built-in on a hard underfloor than it is on a soft carpet and padding.

If you are combining flooring materials, find out who is responsible for the seam between one material and another. Flooring sources that handle more than one material will take the responsibility, as will specialized flooring contractors, who will also hire the correct specialist for each material. Underflooring is best done by the installer; make sure this is specified in the contract. Buying the flooring through the installer will result in the best price. If you are just refinishing a floor, go to a refinisher or restorer who specializes in your floor type.

5. *Wall-treatment installers* include, in ascending order of expense, painters, paperhangers, mirror installers, faux artists, stencilists, and muralists. If you are having a lot of walls painted, the painters can apply the undercoatings for rooms slated for faux treatments or murals at a lower rate than the artists would charge; just make sure the artists specify the undercoatings.

Upholsterers or window-treatment fabricators may install fabric wall treatments, or may be able to recommend specialists; they may also make custom bedding. Wall tile and mirror is also installed at this stage, except when they are to surround built-ins—that comes during stage 6, below.

6. *Built-in fabricators* tend to be cabinetmakers who have a wide range of other crafts at their disposal. They may build an entire unit and finish it themselves, or ship it to a plastic laminate or lacquer specialist. While a plastic laminator or a high-end lacquer shop also can do simpler finishes, it is more cost effective to

---

EVERYTHING AT ONCE?

You can take as long as you like to plan, but once the actual work begins it's better to get it all over as soon as possible—it's messy, it's confusing, and the feeling that it couldn't possibly come together in an aesthetically pleasing whole tends to be depressing. However, there may be one or two instances in which a stop-and-go job is preferable.

The first is when you can't pull together the time or money for the full job just yet, but need extra room immediately. For instance, you just moved and are tripping over things, in which case it might be best to install built-ins right now and put off flooring and window treatments for a year or so. If your home business is about to double its client base, you may have to move some walls and doors, upgrade the wiring, get custom cabinetry for an array of electronic components, slap on any coat of paint, and forget for a while about creating illusions of space or dealing with the rest of your home. However, when a time or money crunch won't let you do the entire job at one time, the work you do get done should fit into your larger space-expanding plan. Then when the time comes to finish the job the plan should just need some minor adjustments.

The second instance applies to people who don't trust their visual imaginations and who need to live with new wall placements for a while, who need to move mirrors around, searching for the most space-enhancing reflections, or who have to have all the built-ins in place before they can even begin to envision floor or window treatments. Some people may need to paint different sections of walls different colors and live with the results over a period of weeks or months before coming to a final decision. These people need infinite patience, and should probably live alone, but the extra time spent can be worth it as long as the experiments take place within a larger, well-thought-out master plan.

- Custom cabinetry is not necessarily more expensive than ready-mades, especially since stores mark up their prices up to 100 percent.
- The most expensive furniture comes from department stores; the same pieces are much more reasonable from manufacturers' outlets.
- You can buy new kitchen-cabinet doors to use on your old cabinet frames.
- With rented sanders, you can refinish wood floors yourself.
- A specialized closet shop will measure, design, and install compact storage for you, but you can also do the planning yourself and buy the components at a hardware store or through a catalog.
- For a large, messy job, consider hiring a handyman to remove all your carpeting rather than let the specialized trades charge you their hourly rate to do it as they move from room to room. You also might be able to hire handymen to haul away demolition debris, but they might not be able to dump it legally; it may be best to include debris removal in the demolition contract.
- If you already own a heavy-duty sewing machine, you can make your own bedspreads and some of the simpler window treatments.
- Licensed plumbers and electricians may seem expensive, but when you factor in the penalties for using unlicensed ones—fines, being forced to undo the job and have it redone, the risk of flood or fire—licensed workers are clearly a bargain.

reserve them only for the finishes they specialize in. Kitchen and bathroom built-ins are best assembled from stock doors, fittings, and hardware; the average shop can order from a wide variety of catalogs and can provide design services. For all built-ins, ask to see the shop drawings so that you can double-check the measurements. Any mirroring or wall tile that surrounds a built-in is generally installed along with the unit.

7. *Electricians, plumbers, and stereo and security installers* return to install wired fixtures, including lighting, dimmers, and ceiling and exhaust fans. If you didn't make arrangements for these before you hired them for stage 2, above, you may find they can't fit you into their schedules now.

8. *Carpet installation*, with the exception noted in stage 4, above, takes place now that the dirtiest parts of the job are completed.

9. *Window treatments* come after carpeting because fit and hang are best judged when all the final flooring is in place. In addition, installing window treatments toward the end keeps them from catching all the dust that rises on work sites. Although it is crucial that the window-treatment fabricators do all the measuring, you can save 10 to 15 percent on fabric if you purchase that yourself. The best deals on blinds and shades are found at shops that specialize in them. For frosted or etched glass, go to a mirror shop.

10. *Schedule furniture deliveries.* Since not every design job can be finished exactly on schedule—for reasons ranging from blizzards or hurricanes to the discovery of a missing stud in an old wall where you wanted to hang heavy art—there's no point in even picking up the phone until you see with your own eyes that the room is ready. Find out if furniture delivery includes unpacking, placement, and removal of the packing materials. If you plan on a number of furnishings from a variety of sources, consider having them all delivered to a warehouse so that you won't continually have to take time off from work. The warehouse will receive the items, check them, report any problems to you, store them, and send them on to you all at the same time. You will pay for this service, but you'll have to hang around waiting only once.

11. *Plant delivery* and placement.

12. *Final touch-ups and cleaning.*

Resources

CABINETRY AND BUILT-INS

Allmilmo Corporation
70 Clinton Road
Fairfield, NJ 07006
201-227-2502
Built-in cabinetry

Aristokraft
P.O. Box 420
Jasper, IN 47546
812-482-2527
Built-in cabinetry

Fieldstone Cabinetry
Highway 105 East
Northwood, IA 50459
515-324-2114
Cabinetry

IKEA
Call for store locations:
215-834-0180
Kitchen and bathroom
    cabinetry, furnishings,
    accessories

Kraft Maid Cabinetry
16052 Industrial Parkway
Middlefield, OH 44062
800-654-3008
Kitchen cabinetry

Merillat Industries
P.O. Box 1946
Adrian, MI 49221
800-624-1250
Kitchen cabinetry

Plain 'n Fancy Kitchens
P.O. Box 519
Schaefferstown, PA 17088
717-949-6571
Kitchen cabinetry

Plato Woodwork
P.O. Box 98
Plato, MN 55370
612-238-2193
Built-in cabinetry

Robern, Inc.
1648 Winchester Road
Bensalem, PA 19020
800-877-2376
Mirrored and lighted
    cabinetry

Rutt
1564 Main Street
Goodville, PA 17528
215-445-6751
Designer cabinetry

SieMatic Corp.
886 Town Center Drive
Langhorne, PA 19047
800-765-5266
Built-in cabinetry

Smallbone
34 East Putnam Avenue
Greenwich, CT 06830
800-765-5266
Built-in cabinetry

Techline
500 South Division Street
Waunakee, WI 53597
800-356-8400
Built-in cabinetry, home office
   furniture

Victorian Millworks
P.O. Box 2987
Durango, CO 81302
303-259-5915
Period-style millwork

Wood-Mode
1 Second Street
Kreamer, PA 17833
717-374-2711
Built-in cabinetry

DESIGN SERVICES

Decorating Den
7910 Woodmont Avenue
Bethesda, MD 20814
800-428-1366
Decorating service

Design Shop
329 Glen Cove Avenue
Sea Cliff, NY 11579
516-759-2705/2706
Decorating service

Imperial Kitchens
1 Piermont Avenue
Hewlett, NY 11557
516-295-9100
Kitchen and bathroom design
   and installation

FLOORING

American Marazzi Tile
359 Clay Road
Sunnyvale, TX 75182
214-226-0110
Ceramic floor tiles

American Olean
1000 Cannon Avenue
Lansdale, PA 19446
215-393-2237
Ceramic and stone tiles

Ann Sacks Tile & Stone
1766A Eighteenth Street
San Francisco, CA 94107
415-864-8585
Stone and tiles

Armstrong World Industries
P.O. Box 3001
Lancaster, PA 17604
800-233-3823
Sheet vinyl, vinyl tiles

Azrock Industries
P.O. Box 696060
San Antonio, TX 78269
210-558-6400
Vinyl tiles

Boen
Route 5, Box 640
Bassett, VA 24055
703-629-3381
Hardwood flooring

Bruce Hardwood
16803 Dallas Parkway
Dallas, TX 74245
800-722-4647
Hardwood flooring

Chicksaw Hardwood Flooring
1551 North Thomas Street
Memphis, TN 38107
800-346-3010
Hardwood flooring

Congoleum
P.O. Box 3127
Mercerville, NJ 08619
800-934-3567
Sheet vinyl, vinyl tiles

Country Floors
15 East Sixteenth Street
New York, NY 10003
212-627-8300
Ceramic tiles

Couristan
2 Executive Drive
Fort Lee, NJ 07024
800-223-6186
Carpeting and rugs

Dal-Tile Corp.
7834 Hawn Freeway
Dallas, TX 75217
800-933-TILE
Ceramic tiles

Du Pont Flooring
Walnut Run
New Castle, DE 19880
800-4-DUPONT
Carpeting

Epro, Inc.
156 East Broadway
Westerville, OH 43081
614-882-6990
Ceramic tiles

Florida Tile Industries
1 Sikes Boulevard
Lakeland, FL 38802
800-FLA-TILE
Ceramic tiles

Hartco
900 South Gay Street
Knoxville, TN 37902
615-4-HARTCO
Wood flooring

Hastings Tile &
Il Bagno Collection
230 Park Avenue South
New York, NY 10003
212-674-9700
Ceramic tiles

Karastan
725 North Regional Road
Greensboro, NC 27425
800-476-7113
Carpeting, area rugs

Kentucky Wood Floors
4200 Reservoir Avenue
Louisville, KY 40213
800-235-5235
Wood flooring

Mannington Ceramic Tile
P.O. Box 1777
Lexington, NC 27293
704-249-3931
Ceramic tiles

Mannington Wood Floors
1208 Eastchester Drive
High Point, NC 27265
800-252-4202
Wood flooring

Marble & Tile Imports
1290 Powell Street
Emeryville, CA 94608
510-420-0383
Stone and tile surfaces

Monsanto Company
1460 Broadway
New York, NY 10036
800-553-4237
Carpeting

National Floor Products
P.O. Box 354
Florence, AL 35631
205-766-0234
Vinyl flooring

Porcelanosa
1301 South State College
   Boulevard
Anaheim, CA 92806
714-772-3183
Ceramic tiles

Puccio Marble & Onyx Co.
232 East Fifty-ninth Street
New York, NY 10022
212-688-1351
Marble and onyx surfaces

Robbins Hardwood Flooring
4785 Eastern Avenue
Cincinnati, OH 45226
800-733-3309
Wood flooring

Stark Carpet
979 Third Avenue
New York, NY 10022
212-752-9000
Carpeting, rugs

Summitville Tiles
P.O. Box 73
Summitville, OH 43962
216-223-1511
Ceramic tiles

Tarkett
800 Lanidex Plaza
Parsippany, NJ 07054
800-367-8275
Sheet vinyl, vinyl tiles, wood
   flooring

Terra Designs
241 East Blackwell Street
Dover, NJ 07801
201-539-2999
Handcrafted ceramic tiles

Walker Zanger
8901 Bradley Avenue
Sun Valley, CA 91352
818-504-0235
Ceramic tiles

Wenczel Tile
200 Enterprise Avenue
Trenton, NJ 08638
609-599-4503
Ceramic tiles

FURNISHINGS AND ACCESSORIES

Baker Furniture
1661 Monroe Avenue NW
Grand Rapids, MI 49505
616-361-7321
Traditional furniture

Bombay Company
Call for store locations:
800-829-7789
Traditional furniture and
 accessories

Brass Bed Shoppe
12421 Cedar Road
Cleveland, OH 44106
216-229-4900
Solid brass and iron beds

Brunschwig & Fils
979 Third Avenue
New York, NY 10022
212-838-7878
Upholstery and drapery
 fabrics

Carole Gratale, Inc.
979 Third Avenue
New York, NY 10022
212-838-8670
Metal-base tables, custom
 furniture

Chadsworth Columns
P.O. Box 53268
Atlanta, GA 30355
800-394-5177
Columns, pedestals, table
 bases

Clarence House
211 East Fifty-eighth Street
New York, NY 10022
212-752-2890
Upholstery and drapery
 fabrics, window treatments,
 wall coverings

Design Toscano
17 East Campbell Street
Arlington Heights, IL 60005
800-525-0733
Columns, table bases,
 pedestals

Dovetail Woodworks, Inc.
114 West Boylston Street
Worcester, MA 01606
508-853-3151
Handcrafted furniture

Drexel Heritage
101 North Main Street
Drexel, NC 28619
800-447-4700
Furniture

Great Meadows Joinery
234 Boston Post Road
Wayland, MA 01778
508-358-4370
Handcrafted furniture

Greeff
210 Madison Avenue
New York, NY 10016
800-223-0357
Upholstery and drapery
 fabrics, window treatments

Habersham Plantation
P.O. Box 1209
Toccoa, GA 30577
800-241-0716
Traditional furniture

IKEA
Call for store locations:
215-834-0180
Furnishings, accessories,
 kitchen and bathroom
 cabinetry

JC Penney
Call for store locations:
800-222-6161
Full line of furnishings

Jennifer Convertibles
Call for store locations:
800-JENNIFER
Sofa beds

Knoll Studio
105 Wooster Street
New York, NY 10012
800-445-5045
Furniture

Laura Ashley Home
Call for store locations:
800-367-2000
Upholstery and drapery
 fabrics, wall coverings,
 ceramic tiles

Lee Jofa
800 Central Boulevard
Carlstadt, NJ 07072
201-438-8444
Upholstery and drapery
 fabrics

Majestic
1000 East Market Street
Huntington, IN 46750
800-525-1898
Fireplaces

Motif Designs
20 Jones Street
New Rochelle, NY 10801
800-431-2424
Upholstery and drapery
    fabrics, wall coverings

Myson
20 Lincoln Street
Essex Junction, VT 05452
802-879-1170
Gas fireplaces

Pier 1 Imports
Call for store locations:
800-447-4371
Furniture, accessories

Puccio Marble & Onyx Co.
232 East Fifty-ninth Street
New York, NY 10022
212-688-1351
Marble and onyx surfaces

Raintree Designs
979 Third Avenue
New York, NY 10022
800-422-4400
Upholstery and drapery
    fabrics, wall coverings

Ralph Lauren Home Collection
1185 Avenue of the Americas
New York, NY 10036
212-642-8700
Furniture, accessories,
    upholstery and drapery
    fabrics, wall coverings

Room & Board
4600 Olson Memorial Highway
Minneapolis, MN 55422
800-486-6554
Furniture

Schumacher
79 Madison Avenue
New York, NY 10016
800-523-1200
Upholstery and drapery
    fabrics, wall coverings

Sears Home Fashions
Call for store locations:
800-948-8800
Furnishings and accessories,
    Kenmore appliances

Shaker Workshops
P.O. Box 1028
Concord, MA 01742
617-646-8985
Shaker furniture

Simmons
P.O. Box 2067
Cerritos, CA 90701
213-404-3888
Adjustable beds, mattresses

Stanley Furniture
Route 57 West
West Stanleytown, VA 24168
703-627-2000
Furniture

Superior Fireplace Co.
4325 Artesia Avenue
Fullerton, CA 92633
714-521-7302
Fireplaces

Taylor Woodcraft
P.O. Box 245
Malta, OH 43758
614-962-3741
Furniture

Techline
500 South Division Street
Waunakee, WI 53597
800-356-8400
Home office furniture, built-in
    cabinetry

Thos. Moser Cabinetmakers
P.O. Box 1237
Auburn, ME 04211
207-784-3332
Traditional furniture

Vermont Castings
Route 107, Box 501
Bethel, VT 05032
800-227-8683
Fireplaces, wood-burning
    stoves

Waverly
P.O. Box 5114
Farmingdale, NY 11736
800-423-5881
Upholstery fabrics, wall
coverings, window
treatments

Wicker Warehouse
195 South River Street
Hackensack, NJ 07601
800-274-8602
Wicker furniture and
accessories

Worthington Group
P.O. Box 53101
Worthington, GA 30355
800-872-1608
Table bases, columns,
architectural details

HOME ELECTRONICS

A/D/S
1 Progress Way
Wilmington, MA 01887
617-729-1140
Home electronics

Bang & Olufsen
1150 Feehanville Drive
Mount Prospect, IL 60056
800-323-0378
Home electronics

Bose Corporation
The Mountain
Framingham, MA 01701
508-879-7330
Home electronics

International Jensen, Inc.
25 Tri-State International
    Office Center
Lincolnshire, IL 60069
708-317-3700
Home electronics

Pioneer Electronics (USA)
P.O. Box 1760
Long Beach, CA 90801
800-421-1606
Home electronics

Sony USA
Sony Drive
Park Ridge, NJ 07656
201-930-7614
Home electronics

Yamaha Electronics
6600 Orangethorpe Avenue
Buena Park, CA 90620
714-522-9105
Home electronics

KITCHENS AND BATHROOMS

Allmilmo Corporation
70 Clinton Road
Fairfield, NJ 07006
201-227-2502
Built-in cabinetry

Alumax Bath Enclosures
P.O. Box 40
Magnolia, AK 71753
800-643-1514
Frameless shower doors

Amana, Caloric, Modern Maid, Speed Queen
Call for information on local
    dealers:
800-843-0304
Major appliances

Amerec/Nasscor
P.O. Box 40569
Bellevue, WA 98015
800-331-0349
Personal saunas

American Marazzi Tile
359 Clay Road
Sunnyvale, TX 75182
214-226-0110
Ceramic floor tiles

American Olean
1000 Cannon Avenue
Lansdale, PA 19446
215-393-2237
Ceramic and stone tiles

American Shower Door
P.O. Box 30010
Los Angeles, CA 90040
800-421-2333
Shower doors

American Standard
P.O. Box 6820
Piscataway, NJ 08855
800-821-7700
Plumbing fixtures

Ann Sacks Tile & Stone
1766A Eighteenth Street
San Francisco, CA 94107
415-864-8585
Stone and tiles

Aqua Glass Corp.
P.O. Box 412
Adamsville, TN 38310
800-238-3940
Heated whirlpools

Aristokraft
P.O. Box 420
Jasper, IN 47546
812-482-2527
Built-in cabinetry

Avonite
1945 Highway 304
Belen, NM 87002
800-AVONITE
Solid surfacing

Briggs Industries
4350 West Cypress Street
Tampa, FL 33607
813-878-0178
Plumbing fixtures

Century Shower Door, Inc.
250 Lackawanna Avenue
West Paterson, NJ 07424
201-785-4290
Shower doors

Chicago Faucets
2100 Clearwater Drive
Des Plaines, IL 60018
708-803-5000
Plumbing fixtures

Country Floors
15 East Sixteenth Street
New York, NY 10003
212-627-8300
Ceramic tiles

Dacor
950 South Raymond Avenue
Pasadena, CA 91109
818-799-1000
Major appliances

Dal-Tile Corp.
7834 Hawn Freeway
Dallas, TX 75217
800-933-TILE
Ceramic tiles

Du Pont Corian
Chestnut Run Plaza
Wilmington, DE 19880
800-4-CORIAN
Corian solid surfacing

Eljer Plumbingware
17120 Dallas Parkway
Dallas, TX 75248
800-42-ELJER
Plumbing fixtures

Elkay Manufacturing
2222 Camden Court
Oak Brook, IL 60521
708-574-8484
Plumbing fixtures

Epro, Inc.
156 East Broadway
Westerville, OH 43081
614-882-6990
Ceramic tiles

Fieldstone Cabinetry
Highway 105 East
Northwood, IA 50459
515-324-2114
Cabinetry

Florida Tile Industries
One Sikes Boulevard
Lakeland, FL 38802
800-FLA-TILE
Ceramic tiles

Formica Corporation
10155 Reading Road
Cincinnati, OH 45241
800-524-0159
Formica laminates, Surrell
   solid surfacing

Franke, Inc.
212 Church Road
North Wales, PA 19454
800-626-5771
Plumbing fixtures

**Frigidaire, Gibson, Kelvinator,
White Westinghouse**
P.O. Box 7181
Dublin, OH 43017
800-537-5530
Major appliances

General Electric
Appliance Park
Louisville, KY 40225
800-626-2000
Major appliances

**Hastings Tile & Il Bagno
Collection**
230 Park Avenue South
New York, NY 10003
212-674-9700
Ceramic tiles

IKEA
Call for store locations:
215-834-0180
Kitchen and bathroom
  cabinetry, furnishings,
  accessories

Imperial Kitchens
1 Piermont Avenue
Hewlett, NY 11557
516-295-9100
Kitchen and bathroom design
  and installation

Jacuzzi Whirlpool Bath
100 North Wiget Lane
Walnut Creek, CA 94596
800-678-6889
Whirlpool baths, personal
  steam baths

Jenn-Air Co.
3035 Shadeland Avenue
Indianapolis, IN 46226
317-545-2271
Major appliances

Kemp George
P.O. Box 182230
Chattanooga, TN 37422
800-562-1704
Designer plumbing fixtures

KitchenAid
701 Main Street
Saint Joseph, MI 49085
800-422-1230
Major appliances

Kohler Co.
Highland Drive
Kohler, WI 53044
414-457-4441
Plumbing fixtures

Kraft Maid Cabinetry
16052 Industrial Parkway
Middlefield, OH 44062
800-654-3008
Kitchen cabinetry

Laura Ashley Home
Call for store locations:
800-367-2000
Ceramic tiles, fabrics, wall
  coverings

Magic Chef
740 King Edward Avenue
Cleveland, TN 37311
615-472-3371
Major appliances

Mannington Ceramic Tile
P.O. Box 1777
Lexington, NC 27293
704-249-3931
Ceramic tiles

Marble & Tile Imports
1290 Powell Street
Emeryville, CA 94608
510-420-0383
Tile and stone surfaces

Maytag Co.
1 Dependability Square
Newton, IA 50208
515-792-7000
Major appliances

Merillat Industries
P.O. Box 1946
Adrian, MI 49221
800-624-1250
Kitchen cabinetry

Miele
22D World's Fair Drive
Somerset, NJ 08873
800-843-7231
Major appliances

Moen, Inc.
377 Woodland Avenue
Elyria, OH 44036
800-553-6636
Plumbing fixtures

Mr. Steam
43–20 Thirty-fourth Street
Long Island City, NY 11101
800-76-STEAM
Steam bath generators, towel
  warmers

Nevamar Corp.
8339 Telegraph Road
Odenton, MD 21113
800-638-4380
Fountainhead solid surfacing

Plain 'n Fancy Kitchens
P.O. Box 519
Schaefferstown, PA 17088
717-949-6571
Kitchen cabinetry

Plato Woodwork
P.O. Box 98
Plato, MN 55370
612-238-2193
Built-in cabinetry

Porcelanosa
1301 South State College
　Boulevard
Anaheim, CA 92806
714-772-3183
Ceramic tiles

Porcher
13-160 Merchandise Mart
Chicago, IL 60654
800-338-1756
Plumbing fixtures

Puccio Marble & Onyx Co.
232 East Fifty-ninth Street
New York, NY 10022
212-688-1351
Marble and onyx surfaces

Robern, Inc.
1648 Winchester Road
Bensalem, PA 19020
800-877-2376
Illuminated and mirrored
　cabinetry

Rutt
1564 Main Street
Goodville, PA 17528
215-445-6751
Designer cabinetry

Sears Home Fashions
Call for store locations:
800-948-8800
Kenmore appliances,
　furnishings, and
　accessories

SieMatic Corp.
886 Town Center Drive
Langhorne, PA 19047
800-765-5266
Built-in cabinetry

Smallbone
34 East Putnam Avenue
Greenwich, CT 06830
800-765-5266
Built-in cabinetry

Stone Products, Inc.
P.O. Box 270
Napa, CA 94559
800-255-1727
Stone wall paneling

Sub-Zero Freezer Co.
4717 Hammersley
Madison, WI 53711
800-222-7820
Refrigerators, freezers

Summitville Tiles
P.O. Box 73
Summitville, OH 43962
216-223-1511
Ceramic tiles

Terra Designs
241 East Blackwell Street
Dover, NJ 07801
201-539-2999
Handcrafted ceramic tiles

Thermador
5119 District Boulevard
Los Angeles, CA 90040
213-562-1133
Major appliances

U-Line Corp.
8900 North Fifty-fifth Street
Milwaukee, WI 53223
414-354-0300
Under-counter refrigerators

Villeroy & Boch (USA), Inc.
5 Vaughn Drive
Princeton, NJ 08540
800-223-1762
Porcelain fixtures, ceramic
　tiles

Walker Zanger
8901 Bradley Avenue
Sun Valley, CA 91352
818-504-0235
Ceramic tiles

Wenczel Tile
200 Enterprise Avenue
Trenton, NJ 08638
609-599-4503
Ceramic tiles

Whirlpool
2000 M-63 North
Benton Harbor, MI 49022
800-253-1301
Major appliances

Wilsonart
600 General Bruce Drive
Temple, TX 76504
800-433-3222
Laminates, solid surfacing

Wood-Mode
1 Second Street
Kreamer, PA 17833
717-374-2711
Built-in cabinetry

LAMINATE AND SOLID SYNTHETIC SURFACES

Avonite
1945 Highway 304
Belen, NM 87002
800-AVONITE
Solid surfacing

Du Pont Corian
Chestnut Run Plaza
Wilmington, DE 19880
800-4-CORIAN
Corian solid surfacing

Formica Corporation
10155 Reading Road
Cincinnati, OH 45241
800-524-0159
Formica laminates, Surrell
solid surfacing

Nevamar Corp.
8339 Telegraph Road
Odenton, MD 21113
800-638-4380
Fountainhead solid surfacing

Wilsonart
600 General Bruce Drive
Temple, TX 76504
800-433-3222
Laminates, solid surfacing

LIGHTING

Broan Manufacturing
P.O. Box 140
Hartford, WI 53027
414-673-4340
Illuminated ceilings

Casablanca Fan Co.
450 North Baldwin Park
  Boulevard
City of Industry, CA 91746
800-759-3267
Illuminated ceiling fans

Con-Tech Lighting
3865 Commercial Avenue
Northbrook, IL 60062
708-559-5500
Track lighting, accessories

Frederick Ramond
16121 South Carmenita Road
Cerritos, CA 90701
800-74F-RAMOND
Lighting fixtures

George Kovacs Lighting
30-20 Thompson Avenue
Long Island City, NY 11101
718-392-8190
Lighting fixtures, lamps

Halo Lighting
400 Busse Road
Elk Grove Village, IL 60007
708-956-8400
Lighting fixtures

Hunter Fan Co.
2500 Frisco Avenue
Memphis, TN 38114
800-252-2112
Illuminated ceiling fans

Illuminations
607 Durham Drive
Houston, TX 77007
713-524-6124
Customized lighting systems

Juno Lighting
2001 South Mount Prospect
  Road
Des Plaines, IL 60017
708-827-9880
Track lighting

Lee's Studio
1755 Broadway
New York, NY 10019
800-LIGHT-57
Freestanding lighting fixtures

Lenox Lighting Collection
100 Lenox Drive
800-635-3669
Lawrenceville, NJ 08648
Lamps

Lightolier
100 Lighting Way
Secaucus, NJ 07094
201-392-3832
Lighting fixtures

Luxo Lamp Corp.
36 Midland Avenue
Port Chester, NY 10573
800-222-LUXO
Lighting fixtures

Philips Lighting Co.
200 Franklin Square Drive
Somerset, NJ 08875
201-563-3000
Light bulbs

Progress Lighting
Erie Avenue and G Street
Philadelphia, PA 19134
215-289-1200
Lighting fixtures

Rejuvenation Lamp & Fixture
1100 Southeast Grand Avenue
Portland, OR 97214
503-230-1900
Victorian reproduction light
    fixtures

Robern, Inc.
1648 Winchester Road
Bensalem, PA 19020
800-877-2376
Illuminated and mirrored
    cabinetry

Studio Steel
159 New Milford Turnpike
New Preston, CT 06777
203-868-7305
Reproduction chandeliers

Thomas Residential Division
950 Breckenridge Lane
Louisville, KY 40207
502-894-2400
Lighting fixtures

MISCELLANEOUS

The Iron Shop
400 Reed Road
Broomall, PA 19008
215-544-7100
Spiral staircases

Life Fitness
10601 West Belmont Avenue
Franklin Park, IL 60131
800-877-3867
Home fitness equipment

Nordic Track
104 Peavey Road
Chaska, MN 55318
800-328-5888
Home exercise equipment

Nutone
Madison and Red Bank Roads
Cincinnati, OH 45227
800-543-8687
Intercoms, remote electronic
    controls

STORAGE SYSTEMS

The Closet Factory
12800 South Broadway
Los Angeles, CA 90061
800-692-5673
Closet organizers

**Closet Maid/Clairson
International**
720 Southwest 17th Street
Ocala, FL 32674
800-874-0008
Closet organizers

Faile Thompson
290 South Arlington Avenue
Reno, NV 89509
800-366-1127
Closet organizers

Knape & Vogt Manufacturing
2700 Oak Industrial Drive NE
Grand Rapids, MI 49505
800-253-1561
Shelving systems

Lee/Rowan
900 South Highway Drive
Fenton, MO 63026
314-343-0700
Closet organizers

Signature Closets
297 Kansas Street
San Francisco, CA 94103
415-626-4657
Closet organizers

Stanley Hardware
480 Myrtle Street
New Britain, CT 06052
203-225-5111
Mirrored closet doors,
    shelving

White Home Products
726 Windy Hill Road
Smyrna, GA 30080
404-431-0900
Closet organizers

WALL COVERINGS

Albert Van Luit
23645 Mercantile Road
Cleveland, OH 44122
800-441-2244
Wall coverings, murals, and
    scenic designs

American Marazzi Tile
359 Clay Road
Sunnyvale, TX 75182
214-226-0110
Ceramic tiles

American Olean
1000 Cannon Avenue
Lansdale, PA 19446
215-393-2237
Ceramic and stone tiles

Ann Sacks Tile & Stone
1766A Eighteenth Street
San Francisco, CA 94107
415-864-8585
Stone and tiles

Benjamin Moore & Co.
51 Chestnut Ridge Road
Montvale, NJ 07645
800-344-0400
Paints

Bruning Paint Co.
601 South Haven Street
Baltimore, MD 21224
410-342-3636
Paints

Clarence House
211 East Fifty-eighth Street
New York, NY 10022
212-752-2890
Wall coverings, upholstery and
    drapery fabrics

Classic Architectural Specialties
3223 Canton Street
Dallas, TX 75226
800-662-1221
Embossed tin panels

Conrad Imports
575 Tenth Street
San Francisco, CA 94103
415-626-3303
Wall coverings, shades

Country Floors
15 East Sixteenth Street
New York, NY 10003
212-627-8300
Ceramic tiles

Dal-Tile Corp.
7834 Hawn Freeway
Dallas, TX 75217
800-933-TILE
Ceramic tiles

Dutch Boy Paints
101 Prospect Avenue
Cleveland, OH 44115
800-828-5669
Paints

Eisenhart Wallcoverings
1649 Broadway
Hanover, PA 17331
800-726-3267
Wall coverings, fabrics

Epro, Inc.
156 East Broadway
Westerville, OH 43081
614-882-6990
Ceramic tiles

Florida Tile Industries
1 Sikes Boulevard
Lakeland, FL 38802
800-FLA-TILE
Ceramic tiles

Focal Point
P.O. Box 93327
Atlanta, GA 30377
800-662-5550
Moldings, ceiling medallions

Fuller-O'Brien
395 Oyster Point Boulevard
South San Francisco, CA
    94080
800-368-2068
Paints

Georgia-Pacific
P.O. Box 2808
Norcross, GA 30091
404-521-4000
Paneling, wallpaper-covered
    plywood

Gercomi Corp.
4474 Northwest 74th Avenue
Miami, FL 33166
305-477-7080
Colored glass tiles

**Hastings Tile & Il Bagno
Collection**
230 Park Avenue South
New York, NY 10003
212-674-9700
Ceramic tiles

Homasote Co.
P.O. Box 7240
Trenton, NJ 08628
800-257-9491
Burlap-covered wall panels

LaBarge Mirrors, Inc.
300 East Fortieth Street
Holland, MI 49422
800-253-3870
Mirrors

Laura Ashley Home
Call for store locations:
800-367-2000
Wall coverings, fabrics,
    ceramic tiles

Mannington Ceramic Tile
P.O. Box 1777
Lexington, NC 27293
704-249-3931
Ceramic tiles

Marble & Tile Imports
1290 Powell Street
Emeryville, CA 94608
510-420-0383
Stone and tile surfaces

Martin-Senour Paints Co.
1370 Ontario Street
Cleveland, OH 44113
216-566-3135
Paints

Motif Designs
20 Jones Street
New Rochelle, NY 10801
800-431-2424
Wall coverings, fabrics

Pittsburgh Corning
800 Presque Isle Drive
Pittsburgh, PA 15239
800-992-5769
Glass blocks

Pittsburgh Plate Glass
1 PPG Plaza
Pittsburgh, PA 15272
412-434-3131
Mirrors

Plygem Mfg.
201 Black Horse Pike
Haddon Heights, NJ 08035
609-546-0704
Wood paneling

Porcelanosa
1301 South State College
    Boulevard
Anaheim, CA 92806
714-772-3183
Ceramic tiles

Pratt & Lambert
75 Tonawanda Street
Buffalo, NY 14207
716-873-6000
Paints

Puccio Marble & Onyx Co.
232 East Fifty-ninth Street
New York, NY 10022
212-688-1351
Marble and onyx surfaces

Raintree Designs
979 Third Avenue
New York, NY 10022
800-422-4400
Wall coverings, fabrics

Ralph Lauren Home Collection
1185 Avenue of the Americas
New York, NY 10036
212-642-8700
Wall coverings, fabrics,
    furniture, and
    accessories

Schumacher
79 Madison Avenue
New York, NY 10016
800-523-1200
Wall coverings, drapery and
    upholstery fabrics

Stone Products, Inc.
P.O. Box 270
Napa, CA 94559
800-255-1727
Stone wall paneling

Summitville Tiles
P.O. Box 73
Summitville, OH 43962
216-223-1511
Ceramic tiles

Terra Designs
241 East Blackwell Street
Dover, NJ 07801
201-539-2999
Handcrafted ceramic tiles

Villeroy & Boch (USA), Inc.
5 Vaughn Drive
Princeton, NJ 08540
800-223-1762
Ceramic tiles, porcelain
    fixtures

Walker Zanger
8901 Bradley Avenue
Sun Valley, CA 91352
818-504-0235
Ceramic tiles

Wall-Tex
180 East Broad Street
Columbus, OH 43215
800-426-7336
Vinyl wall coverings

Waverly
P.O. Box 5114
Farmingdale, NY 11736
800-423-5881
Wall coverings, window
    treatments, upholstery
    fabrics

Wenczel Tile
200 Enterprise Avenue
Trenton, NJ 08638
609-599-4503
Ceramic tiles

Worthington Group
P.O. Box 53101
Worthington, GA 30355
800-872-1608
Architectural details, table
    bases, columns

WINDOW TREATMENTS

Brunschwig & Fils
979 Third Avenue
New York, NY 10022
212-838-7878
Fabrics

Calico Corners
Call for store locations:
800-633-7447
Fabrics

Clarence House
211 East Fifty-eighth Street
New York, NY 10022
212-752-2890
Window treatments, wall
    coverings

Conrad Imports
575 Tenth Street
San Francisco, CA 94103
415-626-3303
Wall coverings, shades

Country Curtains
Red Lion Inn
Stockbridge, MA 01262
800-876-6123
Curtains

Covington Fabrics
267 Fifth Avenue
New York, NY 10016
212-689-2200
Fabrics

Del Mar Window Coverings
7150 Fenwick Lane
Westminster, CA 92683
800-345-3900
Shades, blinds

Eisenhart Wallcoverings
1649 Broadway
Hanover, PA 17331
800-726-3267
Wall coverings, fabrics

Gercomi Corp.
4474 Northwest 74th Avenue
Miami, FL 33166
305-477-7080
Colored glass tiles

Graber Industries
7549 Graber Road
Middleton, WI 53562
800-356-9102
Blinds, shades

Greeff
210 Madison Avenue
New York, NY 10016
800-223-0357
Window treatments, fabrics

Hunter Douglas
1 Duette Way
Broomfield, CO 80020
800-438-3883
Shades, blinds

Kirsch
309 North Prospect Street
Sturgis, MI 49091
800-528-1407
Window-treatment hardware

Laura Ashley Home
Call for store locations:
800-367-2000
Fabrics, wall coverings,
    ceramic tiles

Lee Jofa
800 Central Boulevard
Carlstadt, NJ 07072
201-438-8444
Fabrics

Motif Designs
20 Jones Street
New Rochelle, NY 10801
800-431-2424
Fabrics, wall coverings

Nanik
7200 Stewart Avenue
Wausau, WI 54401
800-422-4544
Blinds

Pinecrest
2118 Blaisdell Avenue
Minneapolis, MN 55404
800-443-5357
Wood shutters

Pittsburgh Corning
800 Presque Isle Drive
Pittsburgh, PA 15239
800-992-5769
Glass blocks

Raintree Designs
979 Third Avenue
New York, NY 10022
800-422-4400
Fabrics, wall coverings

Ralph Lauren Home Collection
1185 Avenue of the Americas
New York, NY 10036
212-642-8700
Fabrics, wall coverings,
    furniture, and
    accessories

Rue de France
78 Thames Street
Newport, RI 02840
401-846-2084
Lace curtains

Schumacher
79 Madison Avenue
New York, NY 10016
800-523-1200
Drapery and upholstery
    fabrics, wall coverings

Shutters, Inc.
9601 Mason Avenue
Chatsworth, CA 91311
818-882-2235
Shutters

Umbra USA, Inc.
1705 Broadway
Buffalo, NY 14212
800-387-5122
Shades

Waverly
P.O. Box 5114
Farmingdale, NY 11736
800-423-5881
Window treatments, wall
    coverings, upholstery
    fabrics